Hanging Out and Hanging On

Hanging Out and Hanging On

From the Projects to the Campus

Elsa Núñez

ROWMAN & LITTLEFIELD
Lanham • Boulder • New York • London

Published by Rowman & Littlefield
A wholly owned subsidiary of The Rowman & Littlefield Publishing Group, Inc.
4501 Forbes Boulevard, Suite 200, Lanham, Maryland 20706
www.rowman.com

16 Carlisle Street, London W1D 3BT, United Kingdom

British Library Cataloguing in Publication Information Available

Library of Congress Cataloging-in-Publication Data

Núñez, Elsa.
Hanging out and hanging on : from the projects to the campus / Elsa Núñez.
pages cm.
Includes bibliographical references and index.
ISBN 978-1-4758-0242-9 (cloth) — ISBN 978-1-4758-0243-6 (pbk.) — ISBN 978-1-4758-0244-3 (electronic)
1. Youth with social disabilities—Education (Higher)—Connecticut. 2. High school graduates—Connecticut. 3. College attendance—Connecticut. 4. Dual enrollment—Connecticut. 5. Eastern Connecticut State University. 6. Connecticut State University (System) 7. Educational attainment—Connecticut. I. Title.
LC4069.6.N86 2014
378.0087—dc23
2014002171

∞™ The paper used in this publication meets the minimum requirements of American National Standard for Information Sciences Permanence of Paper for Printed Library Materials, ANSI/NISO Z39.48-1992.

Printed in the United States of America

Contents

Foreword

"When Need Meets Opportunity"

Jeffrey Bartlett

My role in this story began in 2001, when I retired from the Hartford Financial Services Company following a rewarding career as an information technology executive. Just three days after retiring, I began volunteering at Hartford Public High School and continued in that role for a year. The company was sponsoring philanthropic efforts around the capital city, and I asked it to support my work at the high school, which it did for the next eight years. Since then, I have transitioned into a position as a college specialist employed by the Hartford public school system. Throughout this time, my goal has been to create and manage a College Support Center, a place where we can advocate for and support the college aspirations of inner-city students.

Lack of access to a four-year college education for disadvantaged minority students in America's inner cities is a national problem that severely affects students in Hartford, Connecticut. While the spring 2007 edition of the *Journal of the New England Board of Higher Education* reported that 63 percent of Caucasian students in Connecticut attend college,[1] only 15 percent of Hartford's college age youth do so, and only about 30 percent of the disadvantaged minority students who attend a community college graduate with an associate's degree within six years.

Why is this? In my experience, many students in Hartford have not been taught the value of a college degree; they are often pressured to work while in high school, or they have to quit school entirely to work full-time to help support their families. For others, a higher priority is placed on staying home to care for younger children in their immediate or extended families. Motivation and guidance are often lacking at home, and good students may face ridicule from their peers at school for succeeding academically. Trapped in their urban neighborhoods, they have no sense of the world at large. The results are poor grades, low SAT scores, a lack of understanding of the competitive nature of college admissions, and low expectations for their own academic future.

Early on during my time at Hartford Public High School, Hartford mayor Eddie Perez established a Blue Ribbon Committee to increase the number of Hartford students going to college. It turned out to be an important resource for my work. Estela López, then vice chancellor of the Connecticut State University System, was on the committee. In 2005, I initiated discussions with Estela and her colleague Peter Rosa, a Connecticut State University System trustee and senior program officer at the Hartford Foundation for Public Giving. I felt that too many community college–bound students could not see a clear horizon to obtaining a bachelor's degree, and I asked Estela and Peter if there was some intervention possible that would create a stronger link between community colleges and the state's public universities. The idea was to avoid the stigma often associated with attending community college and to increase students' motivation by giving them a closer affiliation with a state university while they were still enrolled in a community college.

Estela put me in touch with Elsa Núñez, the new president of Eastern Connecticut State University, and she visited our school in fall 2007. It was one of those special, serendipitous days when you get the opportunity to talk to someone with a passion similar to your own about a topic that both of you care deeply about. It was a day when need met opportunity. It was the day that the Dual College Enrollment Program took seed.

At the meeting, my colleague Richard Serrano and I had a list of ideas on how to help our students go to college; one idea was some form of dual enrollment program involving a partnership between a community college and a four-year institution. When Elsa arrived, we were pleasantly surprised to find that dual enrollment was at the top of her own list. However, she wanted to take the idea one step further. She felt that we needed to house the students at Eastern from day one. While Willimantic, Connecticut, where Eastern is located, is only thirty miles from Hartford, life on the campus was going to be light years removed from the impoverished and violent neighborhoods of the inner city.

I remember that we were all very excited and energized that day; Dr. Núñez clearly understood the issues that represented barriers to urban students going on to college. She also concurred with our own view that she should initially focus on one high school versus multiple feeder schools. She said that she would get back to us with a formal proposal, and she kept her promise. A year later, in fall 2008, the first cohort of dual college enrollment students from Hartford Public High School started attending Eastern and Quinebaug Valley Community College's satellite center in Willimantic.

From the start of the program in 2008 to this day, we look for students who have a "spark": young people who are going to value the opportunity. Perhaps they did not do as well as they would have hoped in high school. Family issues and outside distractions may have resulted in a checkered transcript. But they understand the value of education, and they want to go to college, even if they have no plans on how to get there. Occasionally, we have to spend time marketing the idea of going to college to their parents; most of these students have no one in their families who have attended college and, thus, no one to turn to for advice or counsel.

Books about educational programs are often scholarly or technical, lacking the poignancy of the human condition. This book is a welcome counterpoint, providing Dr. Núñez's personal history to portray the people who inspired her, the values that they helped instill in her, and the basis for her professional career and this groundbreaking program. The book also creates a vivid picture of the life of Latinos and other minorities in Connecticut, as well as the alarming gap in academic achievement between low-income urban families and their affluent suburban counterparts. I believe that you will find the firsthand accounts of Dual College Enrollment Program students especially moving and that they can serve as encouragement for other school districts, colleges, and universities to consider similar programs.

I have not seen another program to assist inner-city students in attending college be as effective in meeting that goal as the Dual College Enrollment Program at Eastern. In six years, approximately sixty students have enrolled in the program. Not a huge number, but consider this: perhaps 20 percent of our students at Hartford Public High School go on to college—about sixty students a year. This program adds another ten students, a 17 percent increase in our output. And for each of those students, it is a life-changing experience. Dual enrollment students are enormously grateful for the opportunity to go to Eastern. I hear the following all the time: "I never would have been able to go to college without this program."

At Eastern, Dr. Núñez's leadership and commitment have been fundamental to the success of the Dual College Enrollment Program, but the buy-in has also been evident throughout the campus. While Dr. Núñez provided the vision, it was people such as Kim Crone, director of admissions, Indira Petoskey in the Division of Student Affairs, and Robert Fernandez at Quinebaug Valley Community College who managed and guided the program's early years with extraordinary competence and dedication. Campuswide commitment is essential for this type of program to succeed, along with a similar commitment at partner high schools and local community colleges.

I hope that educators, parents, and other readers find inspiration and counsel in these pages as they seek new opportunities to serve the children of their communities who will become tomorrow's productive and engaged citizens in our democracy. We have a mountain to climb if we are to educate everyone in our society. We must start somewhere, and we need to accept that progress often comes one student at a time. The Dual College Enrollment Program provides an excellent model upon which to grow and expand. Each graduate of the program is a success story—an affirmation of self and an inspiration for all who supported him or her. I

hope that you enjoy reading about these students' struggles and triumphs as much as I have enjoyed being a part of their lives.

NOTE

1. "Trends and Indicators: College Success," *Journal of the New England Board of
Higher Education* (spring 2007), fig. 27, p. 47.

Preface

This book is the story of the Dual College Enrollment Program (DCEP) at Eastern Connecticut State University. Since 2008, the program has enrolled approximately ten high school graduates each fall, students who have either no intention or no clear path for attending a four-year college. They also do not typically meet Eastern's entrance requirements and standards.

In the first semester of the program, students take three or four remedial courses at Quinebaug Valley Community College, conveniently located half a mile down the street from the Eastern campus. At the same time, DCEP students take one course at Eastern and live on campus, fully immersed in the residential life and campus activities that all Eastern students enjoy. Tutoring, advising, and other support services are also available. Each DCEP student is assigned a one-on-one mentor and hired in an on-campus job. By second semester, most DCEP students enroll full-time at Eastern as matriculating students.

Begun in fall 2008 with the first cohort of students from Hartford Public High School, the program was extended in fall 2011 to a small group of students from Manchester High School. In fall 2013, the program expanded to additional high schools in the Hartford area. As of fall 2013, approximately sixty students have been accepted into the program.

WHY DID I WRITE THIS BOOK?

I wrote this book to share the program's growing pains, evolution, and successes with educators, policymakers, parents, and others who are seeking ways to offer the potential of a college degree to inner-city youth. This book is also a tribute to the students who have enrolled in the program and a thank-you to the many people who have worked hard to serve our DCEP students and make this program a reality.

WHO SHOULD READ THIS BOOK?

I hope that educators at the secondary and postsecondary levels who are seeking innovative strategies to increase the college attendance and graduation rates of minority, low-income, and urban students will find this book helpful. There are certainly policy considerations involved in the

DCEP, and I anticipate that local, state, and federal policymakers will find this book useful as they consider ways to improve college access and affordability for underrepresented student populations. Finally, as noted by many people over the years, educational reform can be successful only when entire communities take up the cause. To that end, I hope that parents of school- and college-age students will find this book compelling. I expect that they will appreciate its authentic portrayal of the conditions confronted by Latinos and other minority youth in our inner cities, as well as the possibilities afforded by programs such as the DCEP at Eastern Connecticut State University.

HOW IS THIS BOOK ORGANIZED?

The book starts with two chapters that document my personal and professional journey, which started in the hills of western Puerto Rico in my earliest years and landed me on the unfamiliar streets of Newark, New Jersey, as an eight-year-old. My experiences of overcoming the unfamiliar are reflected in the lives of our DCEP students, and they remind me each day why it is so important to discover new, effective ways of reaching these students.

In telling my personal story of struggle and survival, I especially wanted to share stories of the people who inspired and supported me along the way. I have been determined, throughout the six years since we created the DCEP, to provide students in the program with similar support so that they can be successful.

The next two chapters describe the life of immigrant Latinos and other minorities in Connecticut—stories of discrimination, language barriers, lack of opportunity, hard work, and suffering—and the alarming educational achievement gap that exists today in our state between minority students living in low-income urban neighborhoods and their more affluent white counterparts.

Chapter 5 goes into great detail in describing the DCEP—how it started, how students are recruited, what support services are available, how it is funded, and how students work their way through the program.

What I think is unique to this book, and what I hope engages readers at the most intimate level, are the firsthand accounts of six DCEP students. They come from diverse backgrounds and have a host of issues to deal with. The thread that runs through all their stories is how each has embraced the opportunity of living and studying on a residential liberal arts campus, supported by people who truly care about their success. The transformation that has occurred in these students' lives and the gratitude they express are an affirmation of the program and an inspiration to all those involved.

The final chapter of the book asks the question "How can this program be replicated elsewhere?" and it offers key takeaways for readers' consideration.

ACKNOWLEDGMENTS

I have many people to thank, not only in helping craft this book, but in making the DCEP a dream that is now institutionalized at our university.

People who helped us create and sustain the DCEP include my friends Estela López and Peter Rosa, formerly with the Connecticut State University System; Jeff Bartlett, Richard Serrano, Charlene Senteio, and Adam Johnson and their colleagues at Hartford Public High School; former president Diane Williams and Willimantic Center director Robert Fernandez at Quinebaug Valley Community College; and my many colleagues at Eastern—Rhona Free, Kenneth DeLisa, Kim Crone, Joe McGann, Indira Petoskey, Mary Anne Clifford, Margaret Letterman, Walter Diaz, LaQuana Price, Frederick Hornung, Chris Dorsey, Amilcah Gomes, Kemesha Wilmot, Luz Burgos, Jennifer Holowaty, Greg Ashford, Starsheemar Byrum, Julisa de los Santos, and many others.

Among the generous financial supporters who have helped our DCEP students afford a college education at Eastern are the Hartford Foundation for Public Giving, the Wal-Mart Foundation, the U.S. Department of Justice, the SBM Charitable Foundation, the First Niagara Bank Foundation, and several private donors.

I also want to acknowledge the people who were interviewed for this book, including Eastern faculty and staff, DCEP students, members of the staff at Quinebaug Valley Community College, and the staff and administration at Hartford Public High School.

During my research, I found a number of invaluable historical treatments on the life of minority families in Connecticut, and I am especially appreciative of the works of Ruth Glasser and the Connecticut Humanities Council; Norma Boujouen, James Newton, and the Windham Regional Community Council; Thomas Beardsley; Ron Robillard; Tim Black; the Urban League of Greater Hartford; and La Casa De Puerto Rico.

To the six students who were courageous in sharing their own experiences in the book—Federica Bucca, Maria Burgos-Jiménez, Todd Aviles, Whitley Mingo, Ismael Gracia, and Eshwar Gulcharran—I applaud and congratulate them for pursuing their dreams.

I also owe a debt of gratitude to my four readers who took the time to review and comment on the manuscript. Peter Rosa, Wally Lamb, Dr. Jane Fried, and Jeff Benedict provided invaluable insights and editorial suggestions that I know have improved the final version of the book.

Finally, I need to acknowledge and thank the members of my staff and others who assisted with research and editorial support: Meghan Carden, Amy Brenner-Fricke, Bev Canfield, and Susan Shaloub. I am especially indebted to Edward Osborn, director of the Office of University Relations; his research, interviewing, writing, and editorial support were invaluable, especially in chapters 3, 4, and 12, as well as his contribution of chapter 5.

DEDICATION

This book is dedicated to my mother and father, Juan and Carmen Núñez, who have supported me throughout my life and made huge sacrifices when I was a child to provide me with the possibility of realizing my own American Dream. They taught me to believe in myself, to work hard, to stay humble, and to take advantage of the educational opportunities I was given. I will never be able to pay them back for the sacrifices they made for me and my brothers, but I can return the love that they have given our family since our days in Puerto Rico. I also wish to acknowledge Dr. Morris McGee, my freshman English professor at Montclair State University, whose support and encouragement was a seminal factor in my success at college. Finally, I want to recognize and applaud the more than sixty students who have enrolled in the DCEP since its beginnings in 2008, as well as their families, for having the determination to seek a way out of the endless cycle of poverty and failure in our inner cities. Their courage in coming to a rural campus far from the city streets of their home neighborhoods, their willingness to try unfamiliar things and work hard to achieve their goals, and their commitment to embracing new beginnings as college-educated citizens is a source of pride for our entire campus.

Introduction

The American Dream

Each person born into this world has a story to tell. In the United States, we call that collective story the American Dream, a mythic promise of self-realization cast from the very words of our founding fathers: "All men are created equal." We all have the right to pursue happiness. Political and religious freedoms are unalienable rights established by the very laws of nature.

This basic premise is the bedrock of our democratic society—that all citizens of our great country, armed with their own abilities and sufficient opportunities, can realize their potential and achieve economic and social mobility. It is in pursuit of this dream that we commit to abide by the rule of law and the customs of civilization.

This promise of a better life has brought millions of people from other shores to this land. I am one of those people. A U.S. citizen by virtue of being born in Puerto Rico, I nonetheless came to this country as a young child without the benefit of speaking the English language and with few familiar faces around me other than my immediate family.

Like so many others, my life story has been one of overcoming obstacles and challenges. I was graced by God with good fortune and the support of many people who went out of their way to help me, for no other reason than their own generosity of spirit.

As a university president, I look back today with pride and gratitude that I have achieved much against significant odds. I am ever mindful that, without the opportunities that were made available to me or the kindness of the people who mentored and helped me along the way, I would not be where I am today professionally or personally.

Unfortunately, many people in this country do not have positive stories to tell about their personal journeys. They know that few people want to hear the sad tales they can share. Far too many people in the United States—whether they moved here from offshore lands, are native-born Americans, or are U.S. citizens from the island of Puerto Rico—face a lifetime of poverty, hunger, illiteracy, poor health, and other misfortune. They have not been able to find a pathway out of the ghetto or the barrio. They have not enjoyed the American Dream as I have. They and their families have struggled since the day that they were born to maintain a roof over their heads and find food to feed themselves. A cycle of poverty and neglect continues to be passed from generation to generation in far too many families and neighborhoods in our country. Throughout my professional career, I have sought answers to the question of how to break this cycle of despair.

A MODEL FOR SUCCESS

This book shares my history, starting with my earliest years in Puerto Rico, to provide a context for my professional work. I hope that this expression of my personal survival and success serves to set the stage for the Dual College Enrollment Program, which we have put into place at Eastern Connecticut State University to bring educational opportunity to low-income students from our inner cities.

I also hope that the personal stories of six students in the Dual College Enrollment Program demonstrate what can be achieved when students with potential and determination are given a fair opportunity at success, assisted by support services, and immersed in an engaging, welcoming campus culture and environment. While the scale of the program is deliberately small so that each individual receives the "high touch" service and attention that he or she needs to succeed, we believe that this program can be a model for success in other institutions and communities. Whatever strategy educators and officials in other states and communities pursue, they should do so knowing that the beneficiaries of their work are not only the students whom they serve. Given the changing demographics of this country, the very economic and social future of our nation lies in the balance.

I

Beginnings

ONE

A Personal Journey

El Fanguito and the Flight to Newark

THE SPARK

In recruiting students for the Dual College Enrollment Program, we are not using the typical measures and yardsticks to evaluate traditional college-bound students. If we used SAT scores, class rank, and other standard measures of academic success, most students who eventually end up in the program would not make the cut. What we are looking for and, in fact, what turns out to be the true indicator of success is the indefinable "spark" that Jeff Bartlett references in the foreword.

Think of it as that magical combination of human spirit, personality, and character that gives people the courage to pursue the unlikely and to persevere under the most adverse conditions. While this spark is something that a person is born with, clearly it can be nurtured and advanced through the inspiration of others. In this chapter, I share stories of two such inspirations in my life—my maternal grandmother and my father— to point to the sources of my internal fortitude. Not only have they served to make me who I am and helped me pursue a career path that has led me to my current role as president of Eastern Connecticut State University, each day they also remind me of the spark that we seek in Dual College Enrollment Program students.

CHICKEN SOUP IN EL FANGUITO

I was born in the mountain town of San Sebastián, Puerto Rico, in the northwest part of the island, home to coffee plantations and fruit and dairy farms. The oldest of three children, I spent the first eight years of my life there. While I can remember many things about my early years in Puerto Rico, perhaps the most enduring memory that I have is of our trips to San Juan to visit my maternal grandmother, Ramona. When you are a child, people make impressions on you like a sculptor's fingers in clay, impressions that you only begin to discern and appreciate as you get older. My grandmother's gift to me was a deep appreciation for the value of self-determination, a pride in one's accomplishments, no matter how modest, and an unwavering love of family.

Today, San Juan Bay features sandy beaches, aqua blue waters, fit sunbathers in their sunglasses, and an atmosphere of leisure and luxury. It is lined with marinas sporting an array of luxury yachts and fishing boats. The skyline features a mixture of Spanish colonial buildings and new high-rise hotels. San Juan Bay is a busy waterway, with cruise ships and trade ships bringing more than a million visitors to the island of Puerto Rico each year.

Sixty years ago, when my grandmother lived there, San Juan Bay looked much different. In that era, the bay and the canal mudflats and tidal marshlands that fed it were lined with makeshift shacks, all teetering precariously on stilts over the muddy shallows. This shantytown was known as "El Fanguito," and it was Ramona's home. Like most other people who lived there, my grandmother had migrated to the city from the countryside, where jobs were scarce. She and her eight children shared the slum with seven thousand other families—about forty thousand people.

El Fanguito means "Little Mudhole" in Spanish. It was the largest slum in San Juan, extending from the Miramar Naval Station, along both sides of the Martin Peña Canal, all the way to the bridge in Hato Rey. By the mid-1960s, the government had torn down the shantytown, moving residents to public housing projects. However, in the early 1950s, it was still teeming with humanity.

"Water, water, everywhere, but not a drop to drink" could have applied to El Fanguito. Drinking water had to be carried in with tin cans. Without sewage facilities, people used the water beneath their shacks to urinate and defecate in. Ticks and mosquitos infested the barrio. These unsanitary conditions, combined with heavy rains much of the year, created a chronic dampness, a natural breeding ground for diseases such as tuberculosis, hookworm, and malaria. Children roamed naked and played in the water, undernourished and illiterate. Even in the squalor, there was some form of order, as the shacks were carefully constructed in rows to constitute some semblance of a neighborhood. And throughout El Fanguito, the people exhibited an indomitable spirit, fighting to maintain their dignity as they struggled to survive.

The shacks were made of rough-hewn boards and timbers pilfered by squatters from construction sites or garbage dumps and connected by a maze of footbridges made of planks that hovered on stilts over the mud and water, much as the shanties were. There was no running water and no electricity, and the families that lived there could not even afford kerosene lamps or candles. At night, El Fanguito stood dark and silent, looming over the sewage-infested waters. Each day, the ocean tides would bring the garbage-laden waters back under the shanties; everyone in El Fanguito dreaded the days when the tide was high and the refuse was thrown onto the walkways and footbridges.

It was there in El Fanguito that I would go to visit my grandmother. Ramona was a single mother and still had one of her eight children living with her when we visited. Once we arrived at Ramona's, I felt comfortable, as any child does when in the company of his or her grandparent. But getting to my grandmother's shack was an ordeal each time. As the oldest child in my family, I was tasked with leading the way across the narrow, single-width walkways that constituted the internal "streets" of El Fanguito. The planks were only a few feet off the water and mud, and one false step would result in calamity. The odor was horrific, and the overall effect of the squalor and poverty was oppressive.

I vividly remember the feelings that I had when my parents told me we were going to visit my grandmother, because I was afraid of the trip getting there. For one thing, the planks were loose and narrow, so two people could not walk alongside each other. My mother could not hold my hand, as she was holding my younger brothers. My parents made me walk in front of them, which in retrospect was a good thing because they could see me, as opposed to me being behind them, where I could fall. As I would try to find Ramona's house, my parents would direct me verbally. They would say "turn here" and "turn there," but the houses looked the same to me. I was always relieved when I could step foot inside the safety of my grandmother's humble dwelling.

Ramona built her shack out of "borrowed" boards and other materials. Whatever pennies she had, she used to buy nails to build the house all by herself. I could always sense her pride in what she considered to be her home. I realize now that it was all she had, having toiled and sweated to construct it; that little one-room shack was her pride and joy. She had the same pride in ownership that someone with a much larger home would have, even though Ramona was a squatter without ownership rights, like everyone else in El Fanguito. Nonetheless, my grandmother and the other families who lived there exhibited a resilience of spirit that I look back on today with awe and pride.

My grandmother was a tall, strong woman. She had straight black hair like mine but very long, and she would pull it back into a bun. She had strong features and rich brown skin, just like a Native American. She looked like a Navajo woman, but she was also tall; it was so unusual to see a Puerto Rican woman that tall.

I realize now that she was a survivor, determined to raise her eight children herself in that environment the best she could. She was so proud of the house that she built with scrap lumber. It had one room, with cots on the side where her family slept; they also slept on the floor. In the corner of the room was a wood-burning stove on which she would cook meals.

The biggest climate issue for my grandmother and her family was the humidity in the summer, when the temperature would reach 110 degrees. It was hot and damp. Because people poured liquid waste and solid waste into the water under their shacks, the stench was really bad, especially with the heat and humidity. In those little box houses, it was very uncomfortable for people to sleep. There were no fans, no ventilation at all—just one window and no electricity.

As rudimentary as the shacks of El Fanguito were, once you established your territory, that was your house. My grandmother thought that she was a homeowner, even though she had no bill of sale, no deed. She was a squatter like the other residents of El Fanguito, but she thought that she was successful. She had eight children, but she had a place for them to live and sleep and eat. Even though she knew that she was poor, she took great pride in the fact that she built that house and that she had a refuge for her children—they were not homeless on the street.

One of the ways that Ramona provided food for her children was her chickens. The house was up on stilts, but under the house she had a cage where she raised chickens and gathered their eggs each day. She was so resourceful. My mother is also resourceful, and I think that probably gets passed down through generations. It was all about survival. It was not a matter of pride; my grandmother and her children did not feel like they were special—there was none of that. It was a pride in surviving, pride in taking care of your family.

In addition to observing her perseverance and resourcefulness, visiting Ramona left me with two strong sensory memories. One was the chicken soup that my grandmother cooked in her little home—the best chicken soup that I have ever eaten in my life! She had a little table in the corner where she would put out a bowl of soup for me and everyone else in the family. Usually, the soup had some rice in it, but it was real chicken soup and, for reasons that I am about to explain, very fresh.

I will never forget the first time that I realized how Ramona made her chicken soup. I vividly remember when she turned to me and said, "Elsa, come outside." Everybody else stayed in the house. I think it might have been raining, but she asked me to go outside to help her catch one of the chickens because once she opened the coop, sometimes they would escape. A chicken did come out, and she and I chased it. I thought that it was so much fun chasing the chicken on the planks. And then my grandmother caught it. What I had not realized was that as soon as she picked it up, she broke its neck—it was to be our dinner. That was the first time that I associated the killing of an animal with food. I had not made the connection that the chicken soup we were going to eat was coming from a chicken that she was going to kill. That night, I could not eat the soup. I would not eat it, because I was so scared after I saw her kill the chicken. I never saw her kill a chicken again. I think she realized that I was terrified.

The other thing that the chickens provided the household was eggs, and Ramona used them in many ways. One treat that I always enjoyed was her meringue. She would take the egg whites, beat them, and add a little sugar to make these fantastic meringue desserts. There we were, visiting my grandmother in her one-room shack in El Fanguito to enjoy a big bowl of delicious chicken soup and a wonderful dessert of meringue—you would think we were at the Hilton. She would make an amazing dinner out of nothing—out of nothing because she did not have anything. Every time someone offers me lemon meringue pie today, I always think of my grandmother. She did not have the lemon, so she made only the meringue. But for a child, the best part of the pie is the meringue!

What my visits to Ramona showed me as I got older was how she managed with so little and how she made it so special for me as the oldest grandchild. She was always interested in making it special for her grandchildren. What she could do was modest, but she put herself out to do something special for us every time we came.

Of course, my grandmother was not totally alone. The entire El Fanguito community helped one another. These were not people who were competitive. Most of them were single women with children, with big families. There were not a lot of men around. These were women from the countryside of Puerto Rico. They migrated to San Juan looking for work and looking for opportunity. When they could not find work, when they could not find housing, they decided to build these houses on the water. The shacks of El Fanguito were in place until the late 1950s, when the U.S. federal government came in under Operation Bootstrap. The officials said that the conditions were unsanitary and moved everyone to public housing projects and bulldozed the shantytown. Needless to say, these were difficult times for the families of El Fanguito as they lost their homes, as meager as they were. Those shacks were the only things that they had been able to call their own.

My grandmother developed diabetes as an older woman and died in a hospital in San Juan. I think that the diabetes was a consequence of her diet. People were just not careful with what they were eating, and diabetes in those days was not diagnosed the way that it is today.

One of the important things about El Fanguito was people's answer to their despair. They had nowhere to go and nothing to work for, and so they developed that community as a way of survival. My grandmother's idea that she was a homeowner and had a place to live was an important concept for all the people in El Fanguito. They did not feel that they were a burden. There was no welfare, no Section 8, no food stamps. There was no safety net, so they had to manage their own way.

Each of us can look back to people in our lives—relatives, friends, teachers, employers—people who have inspired us, given us courage, and served as beacons of hope and faith. Sometimes our role models pass along their wisdom through the power of personality or the gift of communication. Others serve to inspire us by demonstrating, through their own survival skills, what it means to be a person of principle and personal resolve. My maternal grandmother was such a special person in my life. I think of her every day. The lessons that I learned from Ramona in her one-room house and on the planks of El Fanguito are still with me. Perseverance, courage in the face of despair, resourcefulness, and an unwavering commitment to family follow me wherever I go.

I did not know it at the time, but Ramona helped give me the emotional tools and inspiration to take advantage of educational opportunities and support presented to me years later. These same values and principles have also served as the foundation of my vision to launch the Dual College Enrollment Program at Eastern Connecticut State University. I have no doubt that the program that is the focus of this book had its beginnings in the mudflats of San Juan Bay, where I learned lessons of dignity and self-determination from Ramona.

THE FLIGHT TO NEWARK

The personal pride and ability to adapt to one's surroundings that my grandmother instilled in me was matched by the sacrifice and hard work that my parents exhibited as we struck out for the promise of a new life. Now that my parents have retired and I have my own responsibilities as a college president, wife, parent, grandmother, and the oldest sibling in my family, I have come to appreciate even more the enormous courage and dedication that my parents had in moving from our small hometown in the hills of Puerto Rico to the bustling city streets of Newark, New Jersey. I can never repay them, but I can continue to honor them by extending their goodwill to others.

* * *

After my parents got married and my siblings and I were born, my father wanted more for his family and decided to move to the United States. He came here in the early 1950s, but my mother and my brothers and I did not come until later. In those days, the man came first, looked for work, and rented an apartment, and then the family followed.

My father borrowed $60 from a man in Puerto Rico to fly to the United States. He was one of about ten men from our town who made the flight, and he was the only one to repay the man who sponsored the trip.

He went to New York first and then to Newark, following a friend who also ended up in New Jersey. I was about eight years old when my father sent for my mother, me, and my brothers. I remember a story that my mother tells that is a great symbol for the transition that we experienced; she has repeated it so many times that I now remember parts of it.

Apparently, I cried and cried when I saw a woman with red hair for the first time. (The owner of the rooming house where we had a two-room apartment had flaming red hair.) I had never seen anyone with red hair, and I was afraid of her. I would say to my mother in Spanish, "What's the matter with her? Why is her hair that color?" It was very strange. My awareness of cultural differences had started for me. Nobody looked like us, and I noticed that right away.

Language was obviously another difference. We could not understand anything that anyone was saying. We were one of the first Puerto Rican families to arrive in Newark, and there was no ESL or bilingual instruction anywhere.

The only thing that helped our situation was people's kindness. We were newcomers and strangers to them, yet people were kind to us. They did not give us money, but they helped in other ways. They knew that we could not speak English, so they tried to tell us where to go and what to do. They taught my mother and father the bus routes. They taught us where the stores were. They taught us how to go to the bank—things that we never would have done on our own. People were very, very kind.

We lived in what is now called a studio apartment. It was all of us in one room. We lived there for at least two years because that was how long it took my mother and father to get enough money to make a down payment for an apartment. In those days, you had to give security money before you could rent a bigger apartment.

I remember trying to read signs. The first sign I read was "Vaconci," and I kept saying "Vaconci," "Vaconci." I kept seeing that sign. I would ask people, "What does 'Vaconci' mean?" and nobody knew what I was talking about. What I was reading was "Vacancy," but I said it with such an accent that no one knew what I was saying.

The first word or saying that I learned in school was "jump rope," because the girls invited me to play jump rope during recess. I did not know what it was. They would hold the rope and say to me "jump rope," "jump rope," and I would say "salta la cuerda," which is the Puerto Rican term. They learned "salta la cuerda," and I learned "jump rope."

My father started off as a machine operator in a factory. A man named Carl Guarino was a foreman in that factory, and he took a liking to my father because of his work ethic. Mr. Guarino left that factory to become the plant manager at Fedders Corporation. When he got that job, he asked my father to go with him. He made my father the foreman. That is where my father's biggest break came from, because his salary went from being that of an hourly worker to a management position.

My father's courage in coming to the United States without English-language skills or a job in hand has never been lost on me. His essential goodness and strong character have served me as constant reminders of the importance of treating all people with respect. He is a humble man, even to this day; yet another lesson that he taught me was to take advantage of opportunities given, earning them "after the fact" through diligence and hard work. The years of sacrifice that he and my mother invested to provide for me and my brothers were an act of love that I can never repay, but those sacrifices have also served as lessons in my own life. Finally, perhaps the most important lesson that my father taught me was his constant reminder that "education is the only way out of the projects."

THE IMPORTANCE OF LANGUAGE

Language was a real issue for me. As the oldest child, I was the first in the family to go to school. It was important that I learn English because I was bringing it home to serve as the translator for the rest of the family.

In elementary school, I was put at a desk in a corner, along with a boy named Darryl. In retrospect, I realize that Darryl was slow and probably had a developmental disability. I remember that he had dark black hair and that all he did all day was draw horses. The teacher would give him big pages of paper to draw on, and he quietly drew horses all day long. He loved to draw horses, and he was great at it—they were beautiful. I was at the other desk because we were both seen as developmentally delayed. The teacher also gave me paper, but I could not draw. I did not know how to draw, so I just doodled. I saw Darryl drawing, so I did stick figures or tried to write the alphabet. I saw what the other children were doing, and I tried to write the alphabet and do what they were doing. I spent an entire year in a corner at a desk, by myself, without any instruction. The teacher saw me as developmentally disabled because I could not communicate. I knew no English. The teacher did not know what else to do.

I try to be understanding today because, as a good historian will tell you, you have to put yourself in the context of the environment around you. It was wrong, but the teacher did not know any better. The teacher was not abusive. She was kind to me, but she did not know what to do with me. And I think that I was disruptive to her in a way because she could not integrate me into her lessons. It was not until two or three years later that another teacher discovered that I could read and write. She gave me something to do, and I did it, and she said, "Oh my God, you can do this work."

I learned English on my own through assimilation. My father always brought home the newspaper, and he would read to me in Spanish if he could get the Spanish paper. He also taught himself how to read English. He could read the English newspaper, not as fast as someone else, but he could read it. He always started with the sports page. I remember that he always told me how all the teams were doing, and then we read the front page together. He read it to all of us.

Because we did not have a lot of other Spanish-speaking families around initially, we kept to ourselves. We went to church on Sundays, but the church and the priest were not welcoming to us. They were not mean, but they did not go out of their way to help us or include us. We went to church, but it provided no connection for us. My mother had no friends. She worked in a factory and could not speak English, so she just did the work. Eventually, other Hispanic women were hired, and some of those women became her friends, but none of them ever visited our home. She separated her work from her family, so our immediate circle of friends was thin. Years later, as more families came from Puerto Rico to Newark, our circle of friends expanded. Some were people whom my father knew from his hometown of San Sebastián, and they became friends of the family. We would have them over for dinner or coffee.

This pattern of families from the same town in the homeland coming to live in the same town in the United States is certainly not unique to people from Puerto Rico. But it was the best support system that we could have. We spoke the same language; we had a common history back in the town where we had lived; and we had a common struggle adjusting to life in the United States. My family and I were slowly creating a new life in this country. Both my parents were working—my father had a great job, considering his lack of education and the barriers of assimilating into a new culture—we had a nicer apartment, and I was seeing progress in my own development.

I was building on my rudimentary English-language skills and demonstrating slowly to my teachers that I had an innate intelligence just as their Anglo students did, which forced them to see me as a real person. My confidence grew as my English-language skills improved, and I was ready for the next step. Armed with the internal fortitude that I had inherited from my grandmother—and supported by the tireless and unwavering support of my mother and father—I was about to embark on an upward path on my educational journey.

TWO

The Dream of College Comes True

None of us get far without the support of others, and even then, such support only matters when we are given a chance to expand our horizons. This chapter continues my personal journey, helping to illustrate how opportunity and support have come together in my life. They have given me the direction and impetus that I needed to pursue a career that led me to be a college professor, an administrator, and now a university president.

A PRICELESS JACKET

As I learned the English language and my elementary school teachers began to see that I had some potential, my father made another huge sacrifice to give me new experiences. He felt that the public schools in Newark were not very good at the time. Since we were Catholics, my father decided to save every penny he had so that my brothers and I could go to Catholic high school. I began to take a bus by myself every day from Newark to Belleville, New Jersey, where I attended the best Catholic girls high school in the state. My father was determined that we were all going to get a good education. He often said, "The only way you will get out of this hell hole is if you get a good education."

I remember one day when I was in high school, my mother and father had the biggest fight that I have ever heard them have. It was Sunday morning, and they were screaming at each other. As I neared the kitchen door, I could hear them arguing, and it was pretty bad. My father said to my mother, "Carmen, I don't know . . . " She was crying, and she said to him, "I can't stand going to church with you anymore with that dirty old jacket. It's embarrassing, and you look so bad."

13

He replied, "I will wear this jacket until the day I die because we have no money for me to buy a jacket. The kids have to go to school."

I turned around and did not go into the kitchen. That was a very profound thing for a young person to hear, because at that moment, I realized that my parents were making huge sacrifices to try to give us a better education and a better life.

"ELSA, I HAD NO IDEA YOU COULD DO THIS!"

I remember feeling distinctively disadvantaged in high school because I did not have fancy shoes or jewelry as the other girls did. The nuns also responded differently to me than they did to the other students. They were very strict and not helpful to me. The other girls in my school were mostly Italian and Irish, and the nuns were sympathetic to them because they knew their families. They did not know my family. I was unfamiliar to them, and like most people, they were uncomfortable dealing with someone with whom they had no prior reference. So I went to school every day with the knowledge that I was diminished in the eyes of the teachers.

I recall two events in high school that were very important in giving me confidence and raising my self-esteem. One was a time in sophomore English class when the teacher gave us an assignment to research a topic and then give an oral presentation on it in front of class. I remember going toward the end of the group. Some of the girls had not taken the project seriously, and they stood there giggling, nervous. The nun was getting angry because she could see that the other girls were not pre-pared.

As I saw them go up, something happened in my mind—I was espe-cially determined to do a good job. When my turn came, I went up with my one little note card, because the nun had said that we could use one. I stood in front of the group and spoke. When I finished, I turned to the teacher and asked her, "Do you have any questions, sister?" And she said to me, "Oh my God, Elsa. I had no idea that you could do this."

It was the first time in high school that I was recognized as a compe-tent student. Up until that point, I was just a number. I was viewed as being one of the girls who did not care. That was the first time that a nun had noticed me.

The second occasion when I made an impression and boosted my self-confidence was in geometry class; it was something that I was good at. One day, Sister Genevieve put a problem on the board, and she could not solve it. She laughed, "Why isn't this working out?" I called out from the back of the room, "Because the equation is wrong." I explained what the equation should be, and she said, "Ok," fixed it, and then said, "That's right, Elsa."

Those were two times when I showed myself and others that I had potential. Even then, the nuns never thought that I would go to college. There were no advisers, no college counselors, and I was not on the list of kids who were expected to go to college. It took another opportune moment to open that door for me.

"DON'T THEY JUST COME AND GET US?"

One day, I was in homeroom with a girl named Susan. She was what we called a "cutup" in those days. She never did her homework. Instead, she would shake me down to copy my homework or beat me up if I did not give it to her. On this day, she was writing something, which was unusual, because she never did any work in homeroom.

"Susan, what are you writing?"

"My college application."

"What is that?"

"I'm applying to college, stupid," she said.

"Oh, you don't have to apply to college," I said confidently.

"What do you mean?"

I explained that college representatives would come to our high school to select us for their respective schools.

"What are you talking about?"

I replied, "The people from the colleges are going to come and take us to college."

Again she said, "What are you talking about?" Now I was uncertain. "Don't they come and pick us up and take us to college?" She said, "No, I went to the library, got these applications, and now I am applying to college."

Up until that time, I had a fantasy that if you were a good girl, if you did well, everyone knew it, and someone would come pick you up and take you away to college. My father did not know how things really worked either. He and I thought that people would select you and take you to college. It is amazing to me now, in hindsight, that I could have been a senior in high school and believe that. We just did not have the family background and knowledge of how things worked that other students had.

"CAN I TAKE THE BUS?"

So I went to the library and started looking at college catalogs. I found a beautiful picture of one campus and decided that I was going to apply to that college. The only criterion that my father had given me was that it be only a bus ride away. I could go to college, but it had to be close enough that he or my mother could take a bus to see me. I asked the librarian,

"Can I take a bus to go here?" and the librarian said, "Yes, you can." It was Middlebury College in Vermont. So I applied to Middlebury.

When my history teacher asked, "Where are you going to college?" I said, "Middlebury."

He said, "You're going to Middlebury? Your father is going to let you go to Middlebury, Vermont?" I said, "Yes, I'm taking a bus."

"What do you mean a bus?"

I explained that the librarian had said that I could take the bus to Middlebury.

"Oh my God, Elsa, no. Middlebury is very far away." Later I found out that Middlebury, Vermont, is five to six hours away from Newark. My history teacher asked what other schools I had applied to, and I told him that I had also applied to Rutgers and Montclair State. He encouraged me to go to Montclair State, which was the most competitive and best state school in New Jersey at the time.

"ELSA, ELSA, YOU GOT IN!"

In those days, letters of acceptance were sent to your house, and copies were sent to your high school principal. All the students received their letters on the same day. There was a long line at lunchtime at the phone booth because the girls at my high school were calling home to see if they had gotten into college. I got on the line with one of my brothers, who had stayed home from work to open the mail. That was how excited my family was.

My brother opened the letter and said excitedly, "Elsa, Elsa, you got in!" I had received acceptance letters from Middlebury, Montclair State, and Rutgers.

The next day, when I got to school, I was called to the office by Mother Superior. She said to me, "I want to know who your father knows." I didn't know what she meant. I said, "Sister, I don't understand what you're asking me."

And then she made it clear; she was angry that I had gotten into college when some of the other girls whom she had been cultivating did not. She assumed that we had connections, which is ironic to me today — because we had no connections!

"DRESSED FOR SUCCESS"

I was proud that I got into Montclair. While Mother Superior was upset initially, in time I received a positive response to my admittance from the nuns and my fellow students. They knew that Montclair was the hardest state college to get into. It had the highest standards. I do not think that I realized at that time how important it was to get into Montclair.

Before orientation day, my mother took me shopping for a new dress. She wanted to buy me something nice, and my father thought that it was a good idea, so we went shopping at S. Klein's, which was like what Kohl's is today. We went into the store, and my mother picked out a blue suit for me. I will never forget it—a two-piece blue suit with a flowered scarf attached to the top.

I tried on the suit and looked in the mirror. I really did not know what to think. In retrospect, I realize that it was a suit for an older woman; it certainly was not a suit for an eighteen-year-old girl going off to college. But I did not realize it at the time. My mother then went to the shoe department, where it had a big flat table of discounted shoes tied together with plastic ties. She made me try on some black patent leather shoes. We got a little pocketbook that was also patent leather; that was the outfit. My mother was so excited.

I was feeling pretty confident until I went to orientation. I took the bus because my parents were working, checked in, and was given a name tag. They said that my big brother—an upperclassman and mentor for the day—was there and would find me.

As I walked in, I instantly knew that I did not belong. The sea of faces around me and the attire of the other students showed me that I was dressed inappropriately. I was like a fish out of water. All the girls had woolen pleated skirts, white blouses with little round collars, a sweater over their white blouse, and a gold round pin with three initials centered on the collar. They had burgundy or black loafers and knee socks. These were upper-middle-class girls with that preppy 1960s look, and I was just mortified. I stuck out like a sore thumb.

My orientation big brother finally showed up. He took one look at me and left; he never came back. It was the most humiliating thing that could have happened to an eighteen-year-old. I was inappropriately dressed, and he did not want to have anything to do with me. That was the end of my orientation.

I got on the bus and went home. I cried all the way home and told myself that I was not going to college after all. This was it. I did not fit in. I did not belong there. I was not going to humiliate myself anymore. I was going to tell my father and mother that I was going to get a job. I got off the bus, walked home, wiped off my tears, and went into the house.

My entire family—my brothers, father, and mother—clamored around me. "How was it?" "Did you have a good time?"

It was supper time. My trip had taken the whole day, and they were excited to hear what it was like. Just as I was going to start complaining, my father said, "We're so proud of you. I know everybody told you that you looked beautiful because your mother bought you such a beautiful outfit."

He had not even seen it; he had gone to work, but he was sure that it had to be beautiful. "I'm so happy that we were able to do that. Your mother used our grocery money for the week." Just as I was going to answer him, my mother said, "Yes, she did look beautiful. She's very beautiful."

My mother had stretched the grocery money the week before so that she could buy me that outfit, because we had no other money. My father was saying that despite whatever we did not have on the dinner table that week, it was important for our family to give me nice clothes to wear to college.

I excused myself to go upstairs to change. As I was walking up the stairs, I knew what I had to do. I knew then that there was no turning back. My family had sacrificed too much for me not to do what they were dreaming I would do. I think that they would have been devastated if I had not fulfilled our dream. I was going to college for my entire family.

FRIENDS FOR LIFE

My freshman year in college was blessed for two reasons—I met two special people that year. I know that I would not be here today if they had not crossed my path.

One day, when I sat down to eat in the cafeteria, a heavy-set woman with a round face and black hair came over to sit next to me. As she did, she spilled her drink on the table. I got up to help her clean the table, and I could tell that she was very nervous. She had no one to eat dinner with, so she had come over by herself and put her tray in front of me. Her name was Gail O'Connor, and to this day, she is my best friend from college. She is my children's godmother, and she comes to every family event. Meeting her was the best thing that ever happened to me at college. Like me, she was looking to make a friend. I also did not fit in. I liked her immediately. She was smart and she knew the ropes. It was wonderful because she helped me through the system. She understood how things worked, and even when she did not, she knew where to go for resources that I did not know existed.

"ELSA MARIA NÚÑEZ—WHAT A BEAUTIFUL NAME!"

The second important thing that happened when I arrived at Montclair State was that I took my freshman English class with a professor named Dr. Morris McGee. He was a World War II and Korean War veteran who had been injured in the Korean conflict and was confined to a wheelchair. He was a Montclair alumnus, a star football player in college, a recipient of a Purple Heart, and a Shakespearean scholar. I did not know it the first day that I walked into class, but I was very fortunate to have Morris McGee for freshman English.

All of us can think of a teacher in school who provided us with unexpected encouragement, mentoring us through difficult times. Professor McGee was such a mentor for me. I would not have made it through freshman year, let alone the rest of my college years and beyond, had it not been for him.

I went into the first class, and Dr. McGee had a policy that girls could not wear pants to class. We all had to wear skirts or dresses. He said, "I'm old-fashioned, and you're not going to wear pants." That was in 1966, and the social revolution really had not taken place yet. I had to find skirts, borrow skirts, because I did not have a lot of clothes. I did not have a lot of money, but I was respectful of his rule and I was always on time.

At the beginning of the first class, he read everybody's name from the roster. He read names like Joe Schmitz, Maggie Johnson, and Cynthia Hawkins, and then when he got to my name, he said with a flourish and with the intonation of someone familiar with the Spanish language, "Elsa Maria Núñez—what a beautiful name!" For the first time, I heard my name spoken like that by an American, by a non-Spanish speaker.

"Elsa Maria Núñez" had a very different sound from William Smith or Teddy Doyle—so my name stood out. Dr. McGee, of course, was trying to make me comfortable.

But I was uncomfortable because everybody looked around, and it was obvious that it was me; I was the only minority person in the room. In fact, I never saw another Latino at Montclair State. But as classes went on, Professor McGee would read my name, and over time, I started to like the sound of "Elsa Maria Núñez." I remember thinking one day when he read it, *What a beautiful name.* Up until that point, I had never thought about my name that way.

Professor McGee was very good, but I was intimidated in class. The other students could all answer the questions. Their analytical skills were quite strong, and they had read a lot of literature in high school. They had read many of the works that we were talking about. I had not. They were also very sophisticated. They were smart, and I was daunted. As someone whose native language was not English, I knew that my writing skills lacked polish and consistency. I was nervous and apprehensive. I never opened my mouth, never answered a question, and Professor McGee never called on me; I just sat there frozen.

Then it was time for our first writing assignment. I wrote an essay, and when I got it back and saw my paper, it was like the day that I walked into orientation and felt out of place. I knew that I did not belong in college when I saw all the red marks on my paper. It was covered. You could not see my handwriting. At the end, it said, "You need to see me in my office." I read that and thought, "Oh my God."

The next day, I went to Professor McGee's office. When I arrived, he said, "Elsa, you are intelligent and you have a lot of potential, but your

writing is very, very poor. The only way you are going to get through this
course is to come to my office every week and work on your revisions."

Thus began my supplemental instruction sessions with Professor
McGee, a time when he taught me how to become a better writer. I spent
hours during my first semester in college, rewriting my essays in his
office. While I was making corrections, Dr. McGee would either be reading a book or correcting papers or writing something himself. I would
rewrite the sentences, a paragraph or two at a time, and then he would
look up and say, "Are you ready?" He would read what I wrote, comment on it, and make me do it again.

Every week I rewrote a paper, because he assigned one essay each
week. So I was in his office all the time. I would write a paper, receive it
back covered with red marks, and then go in to his office and rewrite it.
Professor McGee would give me a grade after I rewrote the paper. He
never gave me a grade for the version with all the red marks on it.

Over time, my writing improved, and I became more confident that I
might actually be able to succeed as a college student. Throughout the
semester, Dr. McGee continued to mentor me and encourage me. Without his steady hand and watchful eye, I have no doubt that my college
days would have been short-lived.

As the semester went on, he would encourage me. He would say,
"Your writing is getting better." He always had a word of encouragement. He said, "I can see that your sentences are more complex. Your
ideas are complex; we want your sentences to be complex." He also
taught me about punctuation. He did not like a lot of fluff. He liked you
to write straightforwardly, explain your ideas. The assignments were all
based on the literature that we were reading, so it was mostly analytical
work.

At the end of the course, I had a solid B, and I was happy to get that
grade. I was the only minority student in a class of middle-class privileged girls, an immigrant whose native language was Spanish—and I had
gained confidence that I could write at the college level.

While Professor McGee was the most important professor that I had in
college, my freshman history professor also was an important person in
my development. Dr. Macaruso gave complicated exams, but I liked him.
He wanted us to use our analytical skills, to analyze current events in the
context of what they meant socially, politically, and economically. It
brought a level of sophistication to my thinking that I had not even considered. He also was complimentary of my papers; as the semester went
on, my writing got better and better.

Gail O'Connor and Dr. Morris McGee were clearly the keys to my
success in my freshman year of college. Socially, I met a friend for life in
Gail, and academically, I met a professor who cared about me, who
wanted me to succeed. In retrospect, I believe that those are the two
ingredients for success in college for anybody who comes from a modest

background. You have got to socially integrate, and you have to be academically supported. If those two things do not happen, you cannot succeed in college.

* * *

The values and spirit instilled in me by my maternal grandmother have never been far from my heart. The importance of education that my father had instilled in me in our early days in Newark, poring over the sports pages of the local newspaper to learn those first few words of English, will also never be lost on me. Finally, the tutoring and support of my freshman English professor, Dr. Morris McGee, was ultimately the boost that I needed to persist at college and eventually graduate. Ramona's spirit, my father's insistence that education was the way out of the housing projects, and Dr. McGee's expert tutelage have guided me to this day and helped inspire me to launch the Dual College Enrollment Program at Eastern Connecticut State University.

II

The Need for Innovative Educational Initiatives

THREE

Tobacco Valley and the Thread City Blues

The Story of Latinos in Connecticut

I was appointed the sixth president of Eastern Connecticut State University on May 18, 2006, and started work on campus in August of that year. Within days, I had the first opportunity to immerse myself in the local community. One of the many wonderful traditions in Willimantic is a monthly street festival during the warm months of the year. "Third Thursday" occurs on the third Thursday of each month between May and September, and it brings street vendors, musicians, acrobats, food carts, nonprofit organizations, and other community members to a five-block section of Main Street, roped off especially for the occasion. Thousands of people throng up and down the street, enjoying the food, entertainment, and good company. In a small town such as Willimantic, it is a time for families and friends to reconnect while enjoying a cultural diversity not expected in a town this size.

I had been at Eastern less than a week when I attended my first Third Thursday. Accompanied by the mayor and a member of my staff, I spent two hours walking the five blocks of the festival. I was truly amazed. The people were warm and welcoming; the cultures on display spanned decades of time and half the globe; and I could tell that Eastern Connecticut State University was held in high regard by the townspeople.

I also discovered something unexpected. Due to reasons that I will soon explain, Willimantic has a large Puerto Rican and Latino community, with some families coming from my own hometown of San Sebastián in Puerto Rico.

I went home that night energized and elated yet curious about how the small town of Willimantic in northeast Connecticut's "Quiet Corner" had developed such a significant, settled Latino community. The 2010 U.S. Census indicated that approximately 40 percent of the overall population of Willimantic was Latino, three times the state average. How did this happen?

I was also soon aware that the Windham School District was one of the poorest districts in the state and that Windham County was the poorest county—and still is. At 11.8 percent, Windham County has the highest percentage of people living in poverty in the state.[1]

All the measures that are used to evaluate the economic and social health of a community—high school dropout rates, home ownership, household income, unemployment—pointed to a community that was challenged to improve the lives of its residents. What were the social, political, and economic factors that had created this cycle?

As I thought about these issues, an unexpected opportunity presented itself. I was asked to give an address in October 2007 at a conference at the University of Connecticut on the history of Puerto Ricans in Willimantic. The year of research and writing passed quickly. As I dug deeper, a picture of struggle and perseverance for Latinos in Willimantic and elsewhere in Connecticut emerged that reminded me of my past. It continues to steel my resolve to this day—to do my part to break the cycle of poverty and unfulfilled dreams that has marked the lives of too many Latinos and other minorities in our state.

* * *

Two-thirds of the students at Hartford Public High School, the main feeder school for the Dual College Enrollment Program (DCEP), are Latino, and almost a third are African American, with a small population of Asians and Caucasians. Although official data indicate that 57 percent of the school-aged population in Willimantic—home of Eastern Connecticut State University and the Dual College Enrollment Program—is Latino (compared to the state average of 16 percent),[2] unofficial estimates put the school-aged population at 65 to 70 percent, reflecting the fact that many Latino residents are undocumented. Given these demographics, understanding the history of the Latino population in Hartford and Connecticut as a whole is important in understanding the social, economic, and cultural factors that influence DCEP students' lives, their family histories, their communities, and their heritage.

With Eastern heavily involved in the life of the Willimantic community, the dynamic in our hometown is also important to understand, for it has influenced the university's relationship with the town for more than fifty years. This brief historical summary provides a context for the life of Latino students as well as a better appreciation for the socioeconomic

realities of our inner cities. We b
of struggle, lack of opportunity
why academic achievement amoı
and African Americans, has been
their parents, and our school syst

LABELS CA

It should be understood that the 1
who live in the United States arı
they see themselves in that way.
U.S. Census Bureau in 1970 for
term to describe people of Latin
shows that some people use the _____ _____, while each label
also appears to have its own regional popularity. For the sake of convenience and clarity, I have chosen to use the word *Latino* exclusively in this
book to describe the various people in our country who would character-
ize themselves as being *Hispanic* or from a Latin American country.

It is important, however, to realize that this word of convenience cannot hope to describe the rich diversity that it labels. There are more than
twenty national groups under the umbrella term *Latino*. We have Latinos
in the United States with American citizenship—Puerto Ricans—and
those who are in the country without legal status. We have Latinos who
are arriving at this very moment and others whose families have been
here for many generations. We have Latinos whose experience is primarily urban and others whose entire experience in this country has been on a
farm or in a rural environment.

While most Latinos share Spanish as a common mother language,
each national group has its own customs, culture, traditions, and history.
That is why a majority of "Latinos" in the United States identify with
their nation of origin, not the pan-ethnic terms "Hispanic" or "Latino,"
and why 69 percent of respondents to a Pew Hispanic Center survey
indicated that they recognized many different Latin American cultures in
the United States, not just one.[3] These recognitions are fundamental to
understanding the unique circumstances of national groups, neighborhoods, and individual people. Because of this complex dynamic, this
brief history of the life of Latinos in Connecticut is meant only to suggest
some of the challenges facing the state's Latin American population and
the context for the work being done in the Dual College Enrollment Program.

CTICUT'S POPULATION GROWTH

the state population grew by only 4.9 percent from
atino population in Connecticut grew 49.6 percent.[4] As
ther states, Latinos continue to be the fastest-growing
population. This growth has also been more rapid among
d children: while 13.4 percent of the state population is Latino,
nt of the K–12 population is Latino.[5]

THE EARLY YEARS

Even though Latinos in Connecticut have been making headlines for their growth in numbers, they have been part of the state's social, economic, and cultural fabric for decades. In the early years, most of them came from Puerto Rico—directly or indirectly—on boats, on planes, by train, and by bus, seeking a better economic future for their families than what they had experienced in their homeland.

In the 1930s, people like Miguel Fernandez came to Connecticut to work in factories such as the New Departure ball-bearing factory in Meriden; salaries there were three times what he was making in San Juan.[6] Gumersindo del Río was one of six men who were recruited to the Winchester Rifle factory in New Haven; he became the first Puerto Rican political boss in New Haven.[7] During World War II, Puerto Ricans came to Connecticut to work for Electric Boat in New London and the munitions factories in Bridgeport.[8] Other jobs could be found in the tanning factories, the hat companies, furniture makers, and other manufacturers in Danbury and surrounding towns.

Following the war and through a relationship between the Puerto Rican Department of Labor and the U.S. Department of Agriculture, migrant workers from Puerto Rico and other Caribbean countries were recruited to do seasonal farm work in Connecticut. They pruned trees in the tree nurseries in Meriden, planted tomatoes on farms in Cheshire, and picked mushrooms in Franklin, only ten miles down the road from Eastern Connecticut State University's campus in Willimantic.[9]

TOBACCO VALLEY

The biggest draw for Puerto Rican migrant workers was the tobacco farms of "Tobacco Valley," which ran from Hartford to Springfield, Massachusetts—more than two hundred tobacco farms covering twenty-seven hundred square miles.[10] They attracted thousands of workers from Puerto Rico. Some workers slept in barns on flimsy cots, fifty to sixty to a barn.[11] Sanitation and plumbing were meager at best. Others, recruited by the Shade Tobacco Growers Association, lived in fourteen camps in northern Connecticut and southern Massachusetts.[12] The camps were surrounded by barbed wire and patrolled by armed guards. Until the 1970s, only the men came up from Puerto Rico. By that time, work was available for women in the curing barns, and entire families ended up living in the camps. As Edna Negrón, who later became an elementary school principal in Hartford, noted, the camps were "barren," with "nothing to do."[13] It was tough, hot, uncomfortable work in the tobacco fields. Néstor Morales, who came to Connecticut from Cataño in 1964, said, "By the end of the day, your back was hurting, your feet were hurting, your knees were hurting. And one time, we found a couple of snakes there."[14]

In addition to difficult working conditions, the contracts signed by the migrant workers were not often honored by their employers. The contracts typically stipulated forty-hour weeks, with a minimum of $1.60 per hour, time and a half for overtime, and three meals a day. The airfare from Puerto Rico was to be no more than $75 and could be paid off by the worker in installments. In reality, workers were faced with twelve- to fourteen-hour days, seven days a week, and no overtime pay.[15] Deductions for airfare, meals, health insurance, and other expenses often took as much as two-thirds out of a man's paycheck.[16]

Other discrimination existed. Edna Negrón was dark-skinned, while her sister was fair-skinned. Her sister's hair was cut in the front of the hair salon, while Edna had to go to the back of the shop to have her hair cut by the "black women." This was in 1958![17]

Puerto Ricans also had to deal with language barriers, and many learned English the hard way—from newspapers, radio, television, and comic books. There was also the residential segregation that continues to exist, with publicly subsidized housing creating Latino concentrations separated from the rest of the communities that Latinos lived in. While Latinos have used these "villages within a town" to provide protection and support to their families, such enclaves also serve as reminders that Latinos are treated differently.

Latinos have also suffered from low expectations. Several years ago, a *Hartford Courant* story described a senior at New Britain High School—I shall call him John—whose parents had come from a small rural community in Puerto Rico. According to the news article, he was thirteenth in a class of more than eight hundred students at New Britain High School, the highest ranking ever achieved by a Latino student at that school. Yet as John described it, "a lot of [teachers] think that if you're Spanish, you're probably not going to be a good student, and you get lumped in like that."[18] John ignored those low expectations and is now on the path toward a career in medicine. His situation is not unique; one Willimantic Latino recalls that during her school years there, "if you couldn't speak English, they would put you in special ed."[19]

* * *

One of the ways that Puerto Rican families faced the obstacles that they were confronting was to invite friends and relatives from Puerto Rico to Connecticut to help share in the struggle. The result was neighborhoods of people in Connecticut cities from the same areas in Puerto Rico. Families from San Sebastían landed in Willimantic. Meriden was the stopping point for many people from Aguada; families from Ponce and Guánica came to Waterbury; and New London was a popular stopping point for people from Ánasco.[20]

In addition to the life of migrant workers in the tobacco fields and other farms, Puerto Ricans and other Latinos found work in the factories. After World War II, Connecticut's munitions and armament factories continued employing Puerto Ricans in New London, New Haven, and Bridgeport. Other jobs were available in the foundries in Guilford, Madison, Clinton, and Union. They worked in Naugatuck (home of Nauga-Hyde!) and in the metal foundries in Meriden and Waterbury.

The hat companies and furniture makers in Danbury were also popular job locations for Puerto Ricans. And it was not just people from Puerto Rico. There is also a large Central American population in Danbury, and people from the Philippines were recruited to New London to work at the Coast Guard base.[21]

MORE PUERTO RICANS COME TO HARTFORD

As the number of farms in Connecticut was cut in half between 1964 and 1979, with some agribusinesses shifting overseas and the remaining farms mechanizing.[22] Latinos who had previously depended on farm jobs for work began to move into Hartford and other cities, seeking higher-paying manufacturing jobs and employment opportunities and joining the growing ranks of Puerto Ricans already there. At that time, almost all Latinos in Hartford were from Puerto Rico, with families following each other in a "chain migration" from the Comerío, Cayey, and Caguas area.[23]

For most of the time since, they and other Latinos have faced a myriad of challenges. For one thing, Puerto Ricans in Hartford faced the same prejudice that they had encountered in the tobacco fields and mushroom farms. Julio Ramirez, a Pentecostal minister from Puerto Rico who was raised in New York City before moving to Connecticut in the 1960s, recounts his experiences in Hartford: "I never slept on the floor in Puerto Rico. I never slept on the floor in Mexico. And I slept in my own country [i.e., the United States] on the floor because nobody wanted to rent to me as soon as I gave my last name, Ramirez."[24]

In addition to facing discrimination, Puerto Ricans and other Latinos moving into Hartford were facing a dwindling manufacturing base: the city lost 26,400 manufacturing jobs from 1963 to 1972, 36 percent of the total.[25] Since then, that trend has only gotten worse in Connecticut. Since 1990, the state has lost 138,400 manufacturing jobs, a staggering 45 percent of its manufacturing base. And while the average weekly earnings of manufacturing employees in Connecticut consistently rank first or second in the country, "'Connecticut cannot compete for low-skilled manufacturing jobs anymore and must concentrate on high-skill, high-paying work centered on advanced technology,' Pratt & Whitney President Davis Hess told state government and business leaders at the 2011 Economic Summit & Outlook in January 2011."[26]

Hartford continues to mirror this statewide trend: the city lost another 23 percent of its manufacturing jobs from 2000 to 2010.[27] The overall loss of manufacturing jobs and the loss of lower-skilled positions are especially troubling for people lacking the requisite skills and education, including basic English literacy skills.

Another factor that negatively affected Puerto Rican and Latino neighborhoods in Hartford and the families who lived there was urban renewal. As manufacturing companies and jobs began to leave Hartford fifty years ago, city planners sought ways to revitalize the inner city. A wave of urban renewal projects, funded largely by federal dollars, swept across the city's North End.

University of Connecticut professor Ruth Glasser points out that Puerto Rican families were displaced from the Clay Hill section in the North End to the Frog Hollow neighborhood in the South Side. As a result, during the 1970s, ten thousand of the city's fifty-six thousand housing units were demolished. "Much of what remained was old or substandard," wrote Glasser.[28]

Tomás Rodríguez, a Puerto Rican living in Waterbury, described the impact of urban renewal on families:

> Urban renewal tore the economic heart out of the community. They broke up the physical and geographical ties that make a community a community. You live in a neighborhood, you feel this is your house, even though you're renting. I remember going into buildings that had doors wide open, it was like one big family. But when you move into a [housing] project, you don't know your neighbors. It's a whole different sense of existence.[29]

Frog Hollow, one of the poorer neighborhoods in Hartford, is a good example of what happens when a family cannot afford to own its home. Ninety-three percent of the residents are renters, 79 percent of whom have moved in the past 18 months. Half spend more than 35 percent of their income on housing.[30]

These economic and social changes have had a dramatic impact on the overall population and demographics of Hartford. Since 1950—the high point in population growth in Hartford when the city had a population of 177,397—"white flight" to the suburbs has mirrored that of other American cities, according to the U.S. Census Bureau. In 1950, 92.8 percent of the population was white, and 7.1 percent was African American. In 2010, census data placed the population of Hartford at 124,775, a loss of 42 percent from 1950. Coupled with this decline in overall population has been a dramatic shift in demographics. In 2010, only 18.7 percent of the city's population was white; 40 percent were African American; and Latinos, who were hardly visible in Hartford in 1950, were 46 percent of the population. Even as their numbers have grown in Hartford, Latinos continue to face high rates of unemployment, poverty, crime, and low educational achievement.

In 2010, Hartford had the second-highest percentage of unemployed Latinos among thirty-eight U.S. cities, at 23.5 percent, with only Providence, Rhode Island, being higher.[31] At 17.8 percent, the city's overall unemployment rate in August 2012 was almost double the state average.[32]

Among cities with more than 100,000 people, the city of Hartford has one of the lowest median household income levels in the nation, which at approximately $30,000, is less than half that of Hartford County. Almost 40 percent of Hartford families with children are below poverty level.[33]

Hamilton Justiniano, a Puerto Rican who moved to Danbury in 1984, describes the economic challenges of inner-city Latino families: "So many Hispanics who have not been able to study and make themselves into professionals, they have the difficulty that sometimes they have to work more than one job, or if they have only one job, they have to work different shifts, they have to take the worst jobs that exist."[34]

While many Latino families have found a way to survive in Hartford's inner city, street gangs and the "easy money" of dealing drugs have become all too familiar a story line. In his book *When a Heart Turns Rock Solid*, Timothy Black tells the story of three Puerto Rican brothers who spent much of their time in the 1990s on the streets of Springfield, Massachusetts, and Hartford. In the winter of 2001, one of the brothers—"Fausto"—who turned to drug dealing to supplement minimum-wage jobs, reflected on his life in and out of jail and rehab: "So many things that I see that are wrong with this society, that are wrong with me, the things that I have done. When is it ever going to stop? When is the cycle ever gonna be broken? Who's going to help us?"[35]

In another interview, Fausto talks about the

> . . . things that have to happen to make a heart turn rock solid. . . . It's poverty. . . . It's a war . . . for any kid to go out there and shoot anybody, there's a series of things that have to happen in his life that he

saw, that he learned, you know, and made him hard, made him finally
say, "in order for me to survive out here, I have to be this way." [36]

Without an education or marketable skills, with the temptations of drug
dealing and petty crimes as a way to survive, and surrounded by street
gangs, far too many inner-city youth find it easy to go down the wrong
path. To them, as was the case for Fausto, it appears inevitable. For those
who stay clean, their lives remain a daily struggle.

AFRICAN AMERICANS IN HARTFORD

This brief historical perspective focuses on the lives of Latinos in Hartford, Willimantic, and other parts of Connecticut. This focus is due to the
fact that the majority of students at Hartford Public High School are
Latino, as well as the prevalence of Latinos in Willimantic, home of Eastern Connecticut State University.

Nonetheless, it is important to note that African Americans in Hartford represent a significant portion of the Hartford population, although
a slightly smaller percentage of the total population than Latinos. Unlike
Puerto Ricans—free U.S. citizens as they touched the mainland shore—
Africans first arrived in Hartford in 1639 as slaves, totaling seven hundred of the city's thirty-eight thousand inhabitants by 1730. At the start of
the Revolutionary War in 1774, Connecticut had the largest number of
slaves in New England—6,464.[37] Following partial emancipation in 1784,
Connecticut abolished slavery in 1848, and African Americans moved
away from the state. In 1900, there were only 1,878 African Americans in
Hartford, but "chain migration" from Georgia and elsewhere increased
that figure to 6,453 by 1930.[38] By 1950, that number had doubled.

Even though there are more African Americans in Hartford now than
in 1950, the increase represents only about six hundred new people annually in the sixty years from 1950 to 2010, when U.S. Census data indicated
that 48,331 African American residents—or 40 percent of Hartford's population—lived in the city.

It is important to note that not all African Americans in Hartford are
the descendants of slaves. The African diaspora has also brought people
with African roots to the United States from the Caribbean and through
other voluntary migrations. These families have had a different, albeit
similar, experience to those families whose ancestors arrived in the United States as slaves.

Clearly, many of the social and economic issues facing Latinos—other
than the obvious one of not speaking English as a native language—are
also being confronted by African American families today, independent
of their family heritage. For instance, while making up 9.3 percent of the
state's population, 19 percent of African Americans in Connecticut were
living in poverty in 2009, and 20 percent did not have health insurance.

Nineteen percent of African Americans in the state did not have a high school diploma.[39]

Chronic unemployment also remains an issue for Connecticut's African American residents. While the fall 2011 unemployment rate for African Americans was a discouraging 15.6 percent, it understated the problem. As a September 1, 2011, report by Connecticut Voices for Children concluded, "it could be that the labor market has become so discouraging for African American job seekers for so long that many have dropped out of the labor force entirely."[40]

Just as Latinos have struggled with prejudice and low expectations, African Americans in Hartford have faced similar challenges. "I think that students of color are automatically stereotyped sometimes when they go into school systems that are predominantly white," said the parent of a student at Capitol Prep Magnet School in Hartford in 2009. "The stereotype that there's no father in the home, that the parents don't care; we have a plethora of stereotypes—that the kids have behavioral problems, that the boys should all be put on Ritalin or something of that sort. Yes, these are definitely issues."[41]

Add to these stereotypes decades of de facto school and residential segregation, racial prejudice, and, more recently, competition with Hartford's growing Latino population for low-paying jobs in the service and retail sectors, and it is understandable why the lack of economic and social progress for the city's African Americans mirrors that of Hartford's Latinos.[42]

THE THREAD CITY BLUES

In addition to the fact that the main feeder school for the Dual College Enrollment Program has been Hartford Public High School, students in the program, like all Eastern Connecticut State University students, are connected to the daily life of Willimantic. The university has been part of the community since 1889, and Latinos have been a major part of the town for almost half the time that Eastern has been there.

Puerto Ricans began arriving in Willimantic as early as the mid-1950s,[43] principally from the western highland towns of San Sebastián and nearby Añasco.[44] At that time, Hartford Poultry Company recruiters from Willimantic began to fly to Puerto Rico to bring back people to work. One of the poultry company's supervisors, Don Cheo, and his wife, Eloa, would loan airfare to the workers, who arrived in town to stay in the Cheo's boarding house, paying $20 a week to live there.[45]

The reasons for the recruitment campaign were several: the company was desperate for workers, and it knew, from observing migrant farmworkers coming to Connecticut, that Puerto Ricans had a strong work ethic and were willing to perform difficult jobs for low wages, if necessary. Puerto Ricans also were U.S. citizens, which eliminated the need for visas. Imagine the social dynamic—groups of people who could not speak English coming to town with a guaranteed job when they arrived.

One worker at the poultry plant, "Rosario," provided some sense of that time in a 1984 interview: "We were 14 young girls who were brought here [from the south coast of Puerto Rico] to work at the chicken factory. The beds were in a line and two of us would sleep in each bed. [Our sponsor would] lock us up to prevent us from leaving the house late at night." Rosario and her friends processed three thousand chickens an hour: "The work was fast and sometimes the girls would cut themselves with the scissors."[46]

"Norberto," a Puerto Rican who came to Willimantic the more typical way—Florida to New Jersey to Connecticut—also worked at the poultry plant. His work consisted of killing forty thousand chickens a day for processing: "I worked there two months; if I hadn't left, I would have died there."[47]

The poultry plant closed in 1972. The other large employer in Willimantic was the American Thread Company, which had a long history in the town. The company was Connecticut's largest manufacturer in the 1880s, and it was known at the time as the Willimantic Linen Company.[48] It is said that one of Thomas Edison's first projects after inventing a commercial light bulb was to supply an "incandescent plant" for the thread company's mill No. 2 so that it could add a night shift.

The thread company was still Willimantic's largest employer in the 1960s, with two thousand workers, and by then, it was also recruiting workers directly from Puerto Rico.[49] As one person in town noted, the American Thread Company "brought planeloads into Connecticut, about 50 or 60 at a time. It got to the point that in some departments, they spoke Spanish only. Only one or two could speak English."[50]

Willimantic's Puerto Rican community also felt culturally isolated. It could not find Spanish-language music records; it had trouble finding familiar foods; and it had to depend on itself to live a normal life. With little education, its workers had scant opportunity to advance in their companies. They were not paid well; they lived in substandard housing; and the benefits of a college education were largely unavailable.

Discrimination also reared its head. The influx of unfamiliar faces and voices in a small rural New England town, jobs in hand, did not go over well with the incumbent population of Willimantic, and one can understand why. In a town of fourteen thousand in 1960, which had seen only a 1 percent annual population growth from 1900 to 1940,[51] any flood of job seekers, let alone people who had already been hired, would be viewed with trepidation. Other ethnic groups struggling to survive in Willimantic—French Canadians, Poles, Irish—were upset. Newspaper reporter Thomas Beardsley, in his 1993 book *Willimantic Industry and Community*, shared the personal testimony of townspeople to reflect the tension at the

time: "We were born and brought up in Willimantic and we were working here. It seems that we should get a better job than those Puerto Ricans. . . . They cut everybody's throat, you know, them Puerto Ricans. . . .
They pushed us out."[52]

As the textile industry in New England changed and the jobs were
sent south and eventually abroad, the American Thread Company's
workforce declined. By 1972, there were only 1,200 workers; in 1984, that
figure was down to 550. The mills closed for good a year later.[53]

WILLIMANTIC TODAY

The city of Willimantic continues to struggle to overcome the loss of the
American Thread Company—the town's flagship employer for more
than a hundred years. At the same time that Windham County is the
poorest in the state, the school district—also one of the poorest—is now
being managed by the state. The Latino community, once almost all of
Puerto Rican heritage, now includes large groups of Mexican and Guate-
malan residents. As stated previously, Latinos make up 65 to 70 percent
of the school-aged population, and literacy remains a central issue in the
education of these children.

The town has yet to find a manufacturer to replace the American
Thread Company—the three largest employers are the local hospital,
town government, and Eastern Connecticut State University. While Latinos sit on the town council and school board, political representation
alone has had little impact on employment, education, and other aspects
of social and economic progress for Willimantic's Latino population. For
instance, 22.8 percent of townspeople live in poverty, and the median
household income in 2011 was 40 percent below the state average.[54]

A LEGACY THAT CHILDREN DO NOT DESERVE

The issues of language, cultural isolation, discrimination, unemployment,
low expectations, and other challenges still remain for Latinos living in
Willimantic, in Hartford, and across Connecticut. Many of these social
and economic forces also affect Hartford's African American community.
These barriers have resulted in a lack of educational progress needed for
low-income urban schoolchildren to achieve economic and social mobility.

The result of this syndrome of social issues is an academic achievement gap between Latino and African American low-income urban students and their more affluent Caucasian counterparts in Connecticut's
suburbs, which is the largest in the nation. Exploring the extent of this
gap and its implications is the focus of the next chapter, "Closing the
Achievement Gap."

NOTES

1. U.S. Department of Agriculture, "Percent of Total Population in Poverty," http://www.ers.usda.gov.
2. Connecticut State Department of Education, "Race and Gender by District," http://www.csde.state.ct.us.
3. Paul Taylor, Mark Hugo Lopez, Jessica Hamar Martinez, and Gabriel Velasco, "When Labels Don't Fit: Hispanics and Their Views on Identity," Pew Hispanic Center, April 4, 2012.
4. U.S. Census Bureau, "State Quick Facts," http://www.census.gov.
5. Bernard Kavaler, "Hispanic Population Increasing, Especially in Schools," Connecticut by the Numbers, http://ctbythenumbers.info, February 4, 2012.
6. Ruth Glasser, "From Rich Port to Bridgeport: Puerto Ricans in Connecticut," referencing Kristin Martin's "Ethnicity, Leadership, and Government, the Struggle for a Puerto Rican Community in New Haven, 1954–1971," unpublished senior essay at Yale University, April 1991, p. 2.
7. Ruth Glasser, "From Rich Port to Bridgeport: Puerto Ricans in Connecticut," in *The Puerto Rican Diaspora: Historical Perspectives,* edited by Carmen Teresa Whalen and Victor Vázquez Hernández (Temple University Press, 2005), p. 177.
8. Ruth Glasser, "Aqui Me Quedo," Connecticut Humanities Council, 1997, p. 35.
9. Glasser, "Aqui Me Quedo," pp. 49, 51.
10. Glasser, "Aqui Me Quedo," pp. 51, 53.
11. Glasser, "Aqui Me Quedo," p. 59.
12. Glasser, "Aqui Me Quedo," p. 53.
13. Glasser, "Aqui Me Quedo," p. 59.
14. Glasser, "Aqui Me Quedo," pp. 41, 55.
15. Glasser, "Aqui Me Quedo," p. 57.
16. Glasser, "Aqui Me Quedo," p. 61.
17. Glasser, "Aqui Me Quedo," p. 97.
18. Matt Burgard, "A Struggle to Beat the Statistics," *Hartford Courant*, October 7, 2007, pp. B1+.
19. Norma Boujouen and James Newton, "The Puerto Rican Experience in Willimantic," Windham Regional Community Council, 1984, p. 47.
20. Boujouen and James Newton, "The Puerto Rican Experience in Willimantic," pp. 77, 87.
21. Boujouen and James Newton, "The Puerto Rican Experience in Willimantic," pp. 89, 91.
22. Glasser, "Aqui Me Quedo," p. 75.
23. Glasser, "Aqui Me Quedo," p. 87.
24. Glasser, "Aqui Me Quedo," p. 97.
25. Glasser, "Aqui Me Quedo," p. 141.
26. Brad Kane, "Connecticut Manufacturing: Fighting an Uphill Battle," *Hartford Business Journal*, February 7, 2011.
27. Mara Lee, "Metro Hartford Still in Top Tier among Manufacturing Regions," *Hartford Courant*, May 8, 2012.
28. Glasser, "Aqui Me Quedo," p. 135.
29. Glasser, "Aqui Me Quedo," p. 139.
30. Partnership for Strong Communities, "Our Neighborhood, Frog Hollow," http://www.pschousing.org.
31. Bureau of Labor Statistics, "Hispanic Unemployment Highest in New England Metro Areas," cited by Algernon Austin, Economic Policy Institute, October 3, 2011.
32. U.S. Bureau of Labor Statistics, City of Hartford unemployment rate, not seasonally adjusted, 2012.
33. http://www.hartfordfood.org/about/importance.html.
34. Glasser, "Aqui Me Quedo," p. 173.

35. Timothy Black, *When a Heart Turns Rock Solid* (Viking Books/Random House, 2009), p. 284.

36. Black, *When a Heart Turns Rock Solid*, p. 267.

37. Dougas Harper, "Slavery in Connecticut," Slavery in the North, http://www.slavenorth.com, 2003.

38. Kurt Schlichting, "Great Migration of African-Americans to Hartford, 1900–1930," presentation at Trinity College, February 8, 2008.

39. Latino Policy Institute, "Overview," an initiative of the Hispanic Health Council, 2009.

40. Keith Phaneuf, "Report Shows Young Workers and Minorities Hit Hardest by Recession Job Losses," *Connecticut Mirror*, September 1, 2011.

41. "Principal's Tough Love, High Expectations Gets Kids into College," http://www.cnn.com, July 22, 2009.

42. In addition to the work of the Amistad Center for Art and Culture at the Wadsworth Atheneum, the African-American Affairs Commission for the State of Connecticut, the Department of African American Studies at Yale University, and the Department of American Studies at Trinity College in Hartford, among the many scholarly works documenting the life of African Americans in Hartford, Connecticut, are "The Negro Population of Hartford, Connecticut," published in 1921 by Charles Johnson, first black president of the historically black Fisk University, and "The State of Black Hartford," published in 1993 by the Urban League of Greater Hartford.

43. The Town of Windham was incorporated in 1692; the city of Willimantic lies within the town and was established in 1893.

44. Boujouen and Newton, "The Puerto Rican Experience," p. 4.

45. Boujouen and Newton, "The Puerto Rican Experience," p. 10.

46. Boujouen and Newton, "The Puerto Rican Experience," pp. 11–12.

47. Boujouen and Newton, "The Puerto Rican Experience," p. 12.

48. Thomas Beardsley, "Willimantic Industry and Community: The Rise and Decline of a Connecticut Textile City," Windham Textile and History Museum, 1993, p. 4.

49. Beardsley, "Willimantic Industry and Community," p. 58.

50. Beardsley, "Willimantic Industry and Community," p. 132.

51. U.S. Decennial Census, http://www.census.gov/prod/www/abs/decennial.

52. Beardsley, "Willimantic Industry and Community," p. 95.

53. Boujouen and Newton, "The Puerto Rican Experience," p. 30.

54. Connecticut Economic Resource Center, "Windham, Connecticut," July 2012.

FOUR

Closing the Achievement Gap

A good education is another name for happiness.
— Ann Plato, a free African American schoolmistress,
Hartford, 1841

Through personal reflections, anecdotes, and historical information, the previous chapter describes the challenges facing Latino as well as African American families in Hartford, Willimantic, and other Connecticut communities. For many families, those challenges have never been overcome. The result has been a cycle of poverty passed down through the generations.

The socioeconomic conditions that led to this recurring milieu in America's inner cities have been well chronicled over the years. In cities such as Hartford, low-skilled manufacturing jobs were exported overseas long ago. Chronic unemployment or low-paying jobs have forced many families to turn every family member, including older children, into a wage earner to survive.

The instability of renting versus home ownership, the high level of teenage pregnancy, and the prevalence of single-parent households further erode the family unit and the support received in the home by children in our urban communities. Poor health and nutritional deficiencies are also harsh realities in the lives of families living in poverty. Outside the home, a world of drug-related gang violence has turned our inner cities into war zones.

This scenario affects the children of low-income urban families from all racial and ethnic backgrounds. What has emerged is a long-standing, continued gap in the academic progress of schoolchildren from these families when compared to students from more affluent families. A recent article in the *New York Times* draws a deliberate distinction between the gap in student achievement based on ethnicity and that based on income level:

> We have moved from a society in the 1950s and 1960s, in which race was more consequential than family income, to one today where family income appears more determinative of educational success than race," said Sean F. Reardon, a Stanford University sociologist and author of a study that found the gap in standardized test scores between affluent and low-income students had grown by about 40 percent since the 1960s, and is now double the testing gap between blacks and whites. In another study by researchers from the University of Michigan, the imbalance between rich and poor children in college completion—the single most predictor of success in the workforce—has grown by about 50 percent since the late 1980s.[1]

While these studies correctly point to socioeconomic status rather than ethnicity or race as the leading determinant in predicting academic achievement, African Americans and Latinos face additional barriers to social and economic equality. Racial prejudice, cultural isolation, and— for Latinos—the hurdles of literacy and language serve as further obstacles to overcome.

Although a preponderance of data demonstrates that the cycle of poverty and low academic achievement dominates our inner cities, it is not exclusively an urban phenomenon. For instance, as much as chapter 3 paints a picture of structural poverty in the city of Hartford, Connecticut, it illustrates a similar cycle in Willimantic, the rural northeast Connecticut town of eighteen thousand where Eastern Connecticut State University is located. This continued struggle for economic and social equality remains a challenge for Willimantic's large Latino population, mimicking the conditions in Hartford and other large cities.

Understanding the "achievement gap" as it has come to be known— that is, the disparity in student academic progress based on family income—is critical to developing strategies for helping our nation's poor break the cycle of poverty and join other citizens in realizing the American Dream. Over the past four decades, educators and public policymakers have worked hard to assess the academic progress of schoolchildren in America, using state and national tests to evaluate student achievement. Today, driven in part by federal No Child Left Behind funding regulations, all states participate in National Assessment of Educational Progress (NAEP) testing, which measures students' academic performance in the fourth, eighth, and twelfth grades in writing, reading, mathematics, and science. The NAEP has been administering its nationally normed tests and gathering and reporting data since 1990.

What has emerged over this time, nationally and from state to state, is a consistent profile in which white suburban affluent students outperform low-income students living in our cities, especially Latinos and

African Americans. Despite billions of dollars in educational funding, numerous reform movements, and a growing recognition that this achievement gap is detrimental to the children that it affects and society at large, the numbers are not improving.

Certainly, not all Latino families are poor, and not all African American families live in our inner cities. Nonetheless, given the demographics and socioeconomics of American cities, including Hartford, Connecticut, the educational achievement gap in this nation is disproportionately affecting low-income minority families living in urban areas.

Why is this occurring? How wide is the gap? What are the implications for Latino and African American students if we do not improve their high school graduation and college attendance levels? How does Connecticut stack up among the nation's fifty states? What impact does the achievement gap have on our state and national economies? And what can we do to improve the performance of students at the lower end of the socioeconomic spectrum?

The achievement gap may be the most important domestic issue facing this nation, more important than any single economic or employment cycle in which we find ourselves. It is fitting to start a discussion about our nation's future with the words of our Founding Fathers. In the Declaration of Independence, Thomas Jefferson and his colleagues wrote that "all men are created equal." In addition to being the political statement that, perhaps more than any other, serves as the bedrock of our democracy, this basic tenet of our society—that we all start life as equals—is borne out by science. Data from the National Center for Education Statistics show that there is no significant statistical difference among ethnic groups for cognitive and motor skills at age nine months.[2] In fact, the data show that at age nine months, babies in this country generally demonstrate the same cognitive and motor skill development, regardless of ethnicity, the educational level of the mother, or income level. At nine months of age, the only factor that seems to make a major statistical difference is the birth weight of the child. Babies who weigh less than they should do not perform as well at nine months.[3]

So imagine a hospital nursery full of healthy babies from all backgrounds—white babies, black babies, brown babies, babies who will go home to mansions, babies who will go home to tenement apartments. Even at nine months of age, they are still operating with similar mental and physical acuity. From there, their paths start to separate; their stars start to glimmer more brightly or dim. Their futures, while not cast in stone, begin to form a predictable path.

The National Center for Education Statistics data set begins to show cognitive performance separation based on income levels by age two, and a gap in cognitive performance is evident on the basis of both ethnicity and income levels by age four.[4] When national NAEP testing of

schoolchildren begins in the fourth grade, the gap translates into significant differences in academic performance in school.

NATIONAL PROFILE OF ACADEMIC ACHIEVEMENT

In 2009 and 2011, NAEP test results showed that African American and
Latino students trailed their white counterparts by an average of more
than twenty test score points on math and reading in the fourth and
eighth grades—about two grade levels. Similar gaps existed in the subject
areas of science and writing.[5] The gap in Connecticut was more than
twenty-five points on each test and for both grades.[6] Equivalent national
data can be seen on twelfth-grade tests in all four subject areas, again
with similar disparities between affluent suburban white students and
urban students of color from low-income families.

National high school graduation rates and college completion rates
reflect this academic achievement gap. According to 2010 U.S. Census
Bureau data and 2011 estimates, while 91 percent of whites in our country have a high school diploma, only 62 percent of Latinos do. The figures
for bachelor's degree attainment are 31 percent and 13 percent, respectively.[7] Eighty-two percent of African Americans have a high school diploma, and 17 percent have a baccalaureate degree.[8]

CONNECTICUT: THE WORST GAP IN THE COUNTRY

In a state of contrasts—the affluence of Greenwich, Darien, and Westport
being only a short drive from the chaotic and violent streets of Bridgeport
and New Haven—it should not be surprising that Connecticut has the
largest achievement gap in the nation. Simply put, the difference between
NAEP test scores of students from more affluent suburbs and those of
low-income students in the state's most depressed urban areas is the
largest among the fifty states.

For instance, as the Connecticut Council for Education Reform noted
in analyzing 2009 NAEP data, the gap of thirty-four points between low-
income and non-low-income students in Connecticut on the eighth-grade
mathematics test is the largest in the nation. Taking science as another
subject area, it was reported in early 2012:

> Scores from the U.S. Department of Education show that on national
> science tests, the achievement gap between low-income Connecticut
> students and their more affluent peers continues to be the largest in the
> nation. The gap between black and Hispanic students and their white
> peers is also one of the worst in the country.[9]

Perhaps the most discouraging set of statistics of all is that as Latino and
African American students in Connecticut move through the school sys-

tem, the gap between their test scores and those of Connecticut's white students actually worsens. For example, the gap between white and presumably more affluent students and their African American and Latino counterparts in Connecticut grew by six and eight points, respectively, in mathematics between the fourth and eighth grades on the 2009 NAEP tests.[10] The gap in reading scores between white and African American students in the same report grew by five points from fourth to eighth grades.[11]

It appears that whereas economically advantaged students, more likely to be white suburban residents, prosper in stimulating school and home settings, Latino and African American children, as well as white students from low-income families living in our cities, are finding neither the motivation nor the support to gain ground.

When test scores are set aside and graduation rates used (the ultimate measure of high school success), socioeconomic and ethnic correlations are both evident. Spring 2011 data from the U.S. Department of Education showed that "the gap between Connecticut's overall graduation rate and the rate for economically disadvantaged students was 21 percentage points—the largest such gap among all the states reporting data."[12]

When ethnicity was compared, "eighty-nine percent of Connecticut white, non-Hispanic students graduated from high school in 2011, compared with 71 percent of black students and 64 percent of Hispanic students."[13] At the same time that Connecticut's overall high school graduation rate of 79.3 percent is above the national average,[14] the high school graduation rate in Hartford is only 59.9 percent.[15] For those Connecticut students from non-English-speaking families, just 53 percent finish high school.[16]

LIFE IN HARTFORD AND WILLIMANTIC

Chapter 3 provides a historical perspective on the lives of Latinos in Hartford and Willimantic, Connecticut. In both communities, low-income Latino students, as well as those from African American families, struggle to achieve academically at rates similar to students in affluent communities. For instance, whereas the gap between low-income and non-low-income students in fourth grade reading on the Connecticut Mastery Test in well-to-do towns such as Avon (10.9 percent) and Greenwich (27.5 percent) reflect their relative wealth, in Hartford, the gap is 36.3 percent, and in Windham, the gap is a staggering 45.6 percent.[17]

The data and narrative that describe conditions today in Hartford and elsewhere in Connecticut for Latino and African American families sound depressingly similar to stories told decades ago. Not much seems to have changed.

Latinos in Hartford

In 1973–1974, when Puerto Ricans made up most of the Latino population in Hartford, they constituted 24 percent of public school enroll-
ments. This represented a huge growth spurt over a short six-year period—in 1967, the percentage of Spanish-speaking students in Hartford
Public Schools was only 11 percent.[18]

How did these students do? "The number of [Puerto Rican] graduates
from Hartford schools who attend open colleges is practically nil," said
Edna Smith, chair of the La Casa de Puerto Rico Board in 1974.[19] The
dropout rate for Puerto Rican students ("Spanish-surnames") was the
largest in Hartford; some estimates ranged as high as 80 to 90 percent of
students entering high school as freshmen failing to graduate.[20]

A 1974 La Casa de Puerto Rico report identified several factors leading to high dropout rates among Puerto Ricans: curriculum that was not
sensitive to the Puerto Rican culture, problems of communication, and
the cultural and language barriers faced by students from rural areas in
Puerto Rico confronting an urban society in a foreign land.[21] On this last
issue, the report also made the point that only 35 percent of Spanish-
surnamed children were in a bilingual-bicultural program in 1973–
1974.[22]

African Americans in Hartford

For African American students in Hartford, the historical lack of educational opportunities and academic success is equally disturbing. In
1994, in the book *The State of Black Hartford*, Marilyn Campbell, former
acting commissioner of education, vividly described conditions for
African American youth in Hartford, who had "the lowest median and
per capita incomes" in the state. "Hartford is also beset with the concomi-
tants of poverty: poor or no prenatal care, teenage pregnancies, poor
nutrition, inadequate health care, substance abuse, AIDS, substandard
housing with lead paint, and street and domestic violence." Added to
these social conditions, Campbell noted two adverse conditions in the
school system. Due to de facto residential segregation, "Black students in
Hartford are isolated from their White peers in suburban districts and
they are also separated from the Puerto Rican majority within their home
district."[23]

Citing data that showed one African American teacher for every
twenty-eight African American students—compared to three white
teachers for every four white students—Campbell concluded, "Not only
are Black students racially isolated from their peers, there is a dearth of
adult images similar to themselves who can serve as role models to
which they can aspire."[24] Campbell also described how state and federal

categorical funding was being used to support remedial and special education programs.

> The pitfall, however, is that these programs tend to be driven by low expectations for student achievement and students are actually taught to these expectations. Consequently, large numbers of children who lack educational enrichment experiences in the home and at school are trapped in an endless web of failure. These negative experiences destroy their motivation to learn, alienate them from school and family, and breed a sense of anomie, fueled by resentment and rage.[25]

Life in Willimantic

Chapter 3 speaks at length about the social and economic conditions that have existed for the sizable Latino community in Willimantic, home of Eastern Connecticut State University. Today, Windham is the only county in Connecticut for which per capita income is below the national average. Windham's per capita income in 2011 was $39,141, compared to the national average of $41,560. At the same time, Fairfield County, in the southwest corner of Connecticut, is the wealthiest metro area in the country, with per capita income averaging $78,504.[26]

Current achievement gap data are especially telling in this rural community, which has a Latino population three times the state average and a school-aged population that is 60 to 70 percent Latino. In the Windham School District, the increase in the achievement gap over time is startling. Fourth-grade students are 30 percentage points below the state average of students performing above goal on the state reading mastery test, 30 points behind on math, and 27 points below the state average on writing. By eighth grade, those figures are 35 percent, 38 percent, and 28 percent.[27]

WHAT ARE THE INDIVIDUAL AND SOCIAL IMPLICATIONS OF THE ACHIEVEMENT GAP?

As a nation whose political system is grounded in fundamental human rights, the United States has a core belief that all should have equal opportunity in the "pursuit of happiness." An educational system that produces the current disparity in academic achievement raises the question of whether or not we will ever truly achieve equal opportunity. Until children from low-income families, especially Latino and African American youth, can dream of being attorneys, doctors, and engineers based on the reality of their own educational performance, those young people will have potential that will remain unrealized.

Let there be no mistake: these students know what they are missing. According to Pew Hispanic Center research, 89 percent of Latino young adults recognize the importance of a college education in achieving social and economic success, yet only 48 percent say that a college degree is part of their plans.[28] While the majority of respondents cited the need to help their families out financially as well as English-language deficiencies as reasons why they do not plan to go to college, the lack of college graduate role models in their families and neighborhoods also reduces the likelihood of attending college.

This legacy of failed potential has a price tag. With the state of Connecticut as an example, if the college completion rates of African Americans and Latinos in Connecticut were that of their white counterparts, those new college graduates would earn an additional $5 billion to $8 billion annually in personal income, and Connecticut would see its state income tax revenues expand by hundreds of millions of dollars.[29]

The value of increasing college completion rates for the disenfranchised is even broader than the financial benefits realized by individual college graduates. The Center for Education and the Workforce at Georgetown University projects that 65 percent of all jobs in Connecticut will require a two- or four-year college degree by 2018.[30] It is also estimated that almost half the members of the workforce aged twenty-five to twenty-nine in southern New England will be minorities by 2020.[31] When all these numbers are considered, it is clear that unless we change educational outcomes, Connecticut and its adjacent states will not be able to maintain their economies over the next decade.

WHAT CAUSES THE ACHIEVEMENT GAP?

The concerns expressed about the achievement gap in this chapter are shared by policymakers and educators at the federal, state, and local levels, who are keenly aware of the challenges facing our school systems. However, the key to any long-term, systemic success that we can have to change the achievement gap is the realization that the lack of academic progress in our inner cities is not simply an educational reform issue. Closing the achievement gap is not just about better pedagogy, improved testing, or more advanced instructional technology. While educators attend to the essential task of improving conditions and outcomes in our classrooms, we must also be willing to confront the fundamental social and economic issues that are the causes of the poverty cycle.

Pedro Noguera, professor of sociology at the Steinhardt School of Culture, Education, and Human Development at New York University, has published several books about the social and economic conditions that have created the educational achievement gap facing our nation today. In a 2010 article, he offered the following insight:

> Over the past 40 years, studies have shown that education policy must be devised in concert with health reform, poverty alleviation initia-

tives, and economic development in order to address the roots of failure in the most depressed areas. From crime and unemployment to teen pregnancy and even racism, education—or the lack thereof—is implicated in many of our nation's social and economic problems. Education can be part of the solution to these and many other problems if reforms are designed and implemented in concert with key constituents—parents, teachers, local leaders and students—and with an understanding of how they must be coordinated with other aspects of social policy.[32]

THE LANGUAGE HURDLE

The symbols of poverty in our nation's cities that Noguera is referencing are all too familiar: urban decay and the loss of manufacturing jobs, chronic unemployment, low-wage jobs, lack of education, single-parent families, gangs and street violence, the frequent moving and instability inherent in renting versus owning a home, nutrition and health issues, cultural isolation, and more. These issues confront our nation's urban poor regardless of national heritage and ethnic background. However, for Latinos, the language barrier must be added to this list, a barrier that cannot be underestimated. This barrier of language may be the most enduring and troublesome impediment to academic success for Latino schoolchildren.

In 2010, almost three hundred thousand people in Connecticut spoke a language other than English in the home; in 49 percent of those homes, Spanish was the primary language.[33] Despite a growing Latino population and the accepted view that English proficiency is essential to academic and career success in this country, bilingual education programs have not kept up with demand.

The advent of bilingual education in Connecticut followed the growing Puerto Rican migration of the 1950s and 1960s. One of the earliest advocates of bilingual education was the legendary Puerto Rican social activist Maria Sanchez, who argued for bilingual education in the public schools and served on the Hartford Board of Education. In 1971, along with educator Edna Negron Rosario, Sanchez led the fight for mandatory bilingual education in Hartford, and in 1977 it became state law.[34]

Today, the state of Connecticut's bilingual education statute requires a bilingual program in any school with twenty or more students classified as having limited English proficiency who speak the same native language.[35] English and the students' native language—most often Spanish—are both used in class. Each student has thirty months to achieve mastery, after which language transition support services are provided, such as ESL instruction (where only English is spoken), tutoring, mentors, summer programming, and other support.[36]

Former Hartford school principal Edna Négrón Rosario has said that thirty months is not enough for English-language learners and that students are processed through bilingual programs too rapidly. While children quickly pick up conversational English, it takes time to learn the "language of science and social studies. . . . Normally we transition three or four years into the program. Research shows that really you shouldn't be doing that until five or six years into the program. Our children transition much more quickly than people recommend."[37]

Perhaps one of the reasons for the quick transition is the lack of bilingual teachers. Statewide, the number of students who speak limited or no English has exploded over the past decade, but the number of teachers trained to help them has actually declined. Eight years ago, one of every twenty-seven students in the state was classified as speaking very limited English; today the ratio is one in eighteen, a net gain of almost nine thousand students.[38] However, since 2005, the number of bilingual certified teachers has dropped 34 percent in Connecticut. At Hartford Public High School's Law and Government Academy, three teachers are certified to provide bilingual education to ninety-three students speaking eight different languages.[39]

This issue of English proficiency for Latino children cannot be overstated. National data suggest that a child who enters first grade without grade-level English-language skills is one year behind the day he or she walks through the door. Citing a study by the National Council of La Raza, Cynthia G. Brown explains, "By first grade, there is a full one-year reading gap between English Language Learners and their English-proficient peers, which grows to a two-year gap by the fifth grade. High-quality preschool opportunities can reduce these gaps."[40]

CLOSING THE ACHIEVEMENT GAP

In the face of the social, economic, and educational issues facing families in our cities, educators and policymakers across the nation are hard at work implementing strategies that can improve educational outcomes and life options for children from low-income families. In addition to policies being implemented by federal, state, and local governments and educational agencies, several private organizations are leading the way in gathering data, funding best practices, and advocating for change on the national stage, including the Achievement Gap Initiative at Harvard University (funded by Harvard, the Bill and Melinda Gates Foundation, and others),[41] the Education Trust,[42] and the Lumina Foundation.[43]

Every strategy that appears to hold promise should be tested, and those that demonstrate effectiveness should be expanded. Some successful strategies that appear to have broad potential include the following.

Community-wide collaboration. In El Paso, Texas, where more than 80 percent of schoolchildren are Latino—chiefly of Mexican heritage—a collaboration involving the University of Texas–El Paso, El Paso Community College, the local school district, the business community, and the nonprofit community is demonstrating what can happen when an entire community is mobilized around the goal of closing the achievement gap.[44]

Structured strategies for parental involvement. The Parents Academy in Miami-Dade County Schools is a national model. Parents receive training so that they can bring paraprofessional-level skills to the classroom when volunteering, in addition to being more involved with their own children's education.[45]

Financial aid programs for minority students to attend college. Since 1995, the Danbury, Connecticut–based Latino Scholarship Fund has raised more than $500,000 in support of nearly four hundred students to attend such colleges as Yale, Boston College, and MIT.[46]

In addition to these selected programs, which show promise for being replicated across the nation, the state of Connecticut—and Hartford and Willimantic communities in particular—are implementing fresh strategies for closing the achievement gap.

STATE OF CONNECTICUT

Under Governor Dannel Malloy's administration, the state of Connecticut is taking an aggressive approach to closing the achievement gap. Governor Malloy's educational reform plan, outlined in the publication "2012: The Year for Educational Reform,"[47] includes several key elements.

Early childhood education. Recognizing the importance of preschool education in developing a child's cognitive, social, and physical development, the plan calls for five hundred additional preschool slots across the state, with additional slots to be funded in future budget cycles.

Intervention in low-performing schools. Based on student performance on standard math, reading, writing, and science tests, twelve hundred Connecticut public schools, including magnet and charter schools, have been ranked with a "school performance index." The lowest twenty-eight ranked schools—"turnaround schools"—will be "guaranteed state intervention and required to have plans to improve student performance."[48]

Support for innovative approaches, including magnet and charter schools. A report by the Connecticut Center for Children's Advocacy showed that spring 2012 test scores for Hartford students attending regional magnet schools, as well as the suburban schools that they were attending as a result of the Open Choice program, were twenty to forty points higher than the scores of students attending regular public schools in Hartford.[49]

Enhanced teaching. The state plan also calls for increasing standards for teaching candidates, incentives to teach in low-performing schools, and other strategies to support teachers.

More time in school. Not a novel idea in countries such as Korea, the basic premise of this strategy is to give students more seat time in class. In a national program announced on December 3, 2012, Connecticut joined five other states to measure the effectiveness of having schoolchildren spend as much as three hundred hours more in school a year. The program started in fall 2013. Participating Connecticut school districts in East Hartford, Meriden, and New London can decide whether that means Saturday classes, longer school days, or longer school years. Funding is from the Ford Foundation and the National Center on Time & Learning in Boston.[50]

Hartford Public Schools. A three-year, $5 million grant from the Bill and Melinda Gates Foundation was announced on December 5, 2012, and it will support two charter school networks in Hartford. The Achievement First charter network will receive funding to train future principals through a leadership academy, while the Jumoke Academy will receive funds to manage two additional charter schools by 2015.[51]

Town of Windham/Willimantic. The Windham School District is one of the districts being managed by the state. The district has developed a three-year "strategic operating plan," which includes six goals and such strategies as creating two separate academies at Windham High School; developing a magnet school; enhancing teacher quality; improving special education, preschool, and English-language learner services; lengthening the school day; reducing student truancy; and expanding parent involvement.[52]

* * *

While chapter 3 presents a historical perspective on the lives of Latinos and African Americans in Connecticut—especially in Willimantic, home of Eastern Connecticut State University, and Hartford, where several feeder high schools for the Dual College Enrollment Program are located—the purpose of this chapter has been to establish the need for social and educational reform and action.

My personal experiences as a young Puerto Rican living in Newark, New Jersey—of struggle, prejudice, and moments of despair—have echoed across the Latino experience in Connecticut over the past fifty years. Those experiences reverberate even today in the neighborhoods of Hartford and Willimantic. Nonetheless, this chapter on the achievement gap—the disparity in educational progress among Connecticut's schoolchildren—is not an attempt to criticize or place blame. In our American democracy, we all share the responsibility of improving the social conditions found in our neighborhoods and schools, regardless of where we live and where those conditions exist. We share the social and political institutions that have been created to ensure opportunity for all. We also share in the current economic conditions that continue to threaten the delivery of essential social and educational services across the nation.

The need to erase the achievement gap in Connecticut and beyond is readily acknowledged by educators and public officials, and many people are working diligently every day to make a difference in the lives of children at the bottom of the achievement spectrum, even as public resources are being stretched and reduced.

We cannot fix the ills of society overnight, nor can we turn decades of lost opportunities around with good intentions alone. In the end, we can only do what we do best. In my case, that has been to look internally at our resources on the Eastern Connecticut State University campus to see what we can do for our local townspeople and students from other communities. We recognize, as Pedro Noguera has noted, that the achievement gap is not solely an educational reform issue. To that end, Eastern worked closely with the local school district to enhance preschool literacy through a three-year, $3.9 million Early Reading Grant from the U.S. Department of Education to provide English-language instruction to six hundred Windham preschoolers and provide professional development to their teachers. Although the grant has ended, the university will continue working with the local school district on this critically important initiative. Through our academic departments and our Center for Community Engagement, more than one thousand Eastern students also tutor and provide other support in local schools, including staffing an intensive tutoring program for Latino children in Windham Middle School.

We have also turned our attention to the urban neighborhoods of Hartford and Manchester, where the poverty cycle and the lack of educational progress demand special attention. To help inner-city students reach out and grasp the dream of a college education, we have created the Dual College Enrollment Program. This is our contribution to breaking the poverty cycle at the stage where it may matter most—as young Latinos and African Americans, as well as white students from low-income families, reach adulthood. Access to and success in college is truly the "fork in the road." If we can find a way to place students in a new, supportive environment where they can witness their own success, perhaps we can short-circuit the negative role models and disruptive forces in their lives sufficient to place them on a better path. Like all Americans, they deserve the opportunity to become educated members of their communities, living rewarding lives while making a positive difference in their home neighborhoods.

NOTES

1. Sabrina Tavernise, "Rich and Poor Further Apart in Education," *New York Times*, February 10, 2012, pp. A1+.

2. National Center for Education Statistics, "The Condition of Education 2009" (No. 2009-081), 2009, indicator 3.

3. National Center for Education Statistics, Early Childhood Longitudinal Study, birth cohort 9 months to kindergarten, 2007; see Table 119 (prepared in December 2010); also http://nces.ed.gov.ecls/birth.asp.

4. National Center for Education Statistics, Early Childhood Longitudinal Study.

5. National Center for Education Statistics, "NAEP State Comparisons," http://nces.ed.gov/nationsreportcard/statecomparisons.

6. National Center for Education Statistics, "NAEP State Comparisons."

7. Office of Minority Health, "Hispanic/Latino Profile," September 7, 2012.

8. U.S. Census Bureau 2009 estimates as reported by Alex Richards, "Census Data Show Rise in College Degrees, but Also in Racial Gaps in Education," *Chronicle of Higher Education*, January 23, 2011.

9. Jacqueline Rabe Thomas, "Education Report Card: Achievement Gap Lingers," *Connecticut Mirror*, May 10, 2012.

10. National Center for Education Statistics, "NAEP State Comparisons."

11. National Center for Education Statistics, "NAEP State Comparisons."

12. Kathleen Megan, "State Has Largest Disparity in Graduation Rates," *Hartford Courant*, November 27, 2012.

13. Megan, "State Has Largest Disparity."

14. Commissioner Mark McQuillan, "2009 Connecticut Adjusted Cohort Graduation Rates," Connecticut Department of Education, March 23, 2010.

15. "Hartford Public School District: 2011 CMT and CAPT Test Results: A Summary," Achieve Hartford, http://www.achievehartford.org, October 3, 2011.

16. Robert Frahm, "New Tracking System Shows Troubling Graduation Rates for Minority Students," *Connecticut Mirror*, March 24, 2010.

17. Connecticut Council for Education Reform, "What Is the Gap?" http://www.ctedreform.org, 2012.

18. Adriana Falcone, social worker for the Lincoln Institute, University of Hartford, "A Study of Educational Opportunities for the Spanish Speaking in Hartford," La Casa de Puerto Rico, October 24, 1974, pp. 4.

19. Falcone, "A Study of Educational Opportunities," foreword.

20. Falcone, "A Study of Educational Opportunities," pp. 16–17.

21. Falcone, "A Study of Educational Opportunities," p. 19.

22. Falcone, "A Study of Educational Opportunities," p. 29.

23. Marilyn Campbell, "Public Education in Hartford, Connecticut," in *The State of Black Hartford*, edited by Stanley Battle (Urban League of Greater Hartford, June 1994), pp. 102–3.

24. Campbell, "Public Education."

25. Campbell, "Public Education."

26. Mara Lee, "Metro Hartford's Wealth on Upswing," *Hartford Courant*, November 27, 2012, p. A11.

27. Connecticut Economic Resource Center, "Windham Town Profile," July 2012, p. 1.

28. Mark Hugo Lopez, "Latinos and Education: Explaining the Attainment Gap," Pew Hispanic Center, http://www.pewhispanic.org/2009/10/07/latinos-and-education-explaining-the-attainment-gap, October 7, 2009.

29. McKinsey & Co., "The Impact of the Achievement Gap in America's Schools," April 2009, p. 6.

30. Anthony P. Carnevale, Nicole Smith, and Jeff Strohl, "Help Wanted," a report by the Georgetown University Center on Education and the Workforce, Georgetown Public Policy Institute, June 15, 2010.

31. Stephen Coelen and Joseph Berger, "New England 2020: A Forecast of Educational Attainment and Its Implications for the Workforce of the New England States," June 2006.

32. Pedro Noguera, "A New Vision of School Reform," *The Nation*, http://www.thenation.com/article/new-vision-school-reform#, June 14, 2010.

33. Migration Policy Institute, "Connecticut Language and Education," http://www.migrationinformation.org, 2010.

34. Connecticut Women's Hall of Fame, http://cwhf.org/inductees/politics-government-law/maria-c-sanchez, 2012.

35. While Spanish is by far the most prevalent language spoken by English-language learners in Connecticut, Vietnamese, Polish, Chinese, and Portuguese were also evident in large numbers.

36. Connecticut Department of Education, "The Bilingual Education Statute," 2010.

37. Ruth Glasser, "Aqui Me Quedo," Connecticut Humanities Council, 1997, p. 171

38. Jacqueline Rabe Thomas, "Lack of Teachers Hampers Education of Non-English Speakers," *Connecticut Mirror*, October 20, 2010.

39. Rabe Thomas, "Lack of Teachers."

40. Cynthia G. Brown, "Pre-school and ELT for ELLs," National Journal.com, August 27, 2012, http://education.nationaljournal.com/2012/08/kids-learning-language.php.

41. See http://www.agi.harvard.edu for more information.

42. See http://www.edtrust.org for more information.

43. See http://www.luminafoundation.org for more information.

44. See http://www.epcae.org for more information.

45. See http://theparentacademy.dadeschools.net for more information.

46. See http://www.danburylatinofund.com for more information.

47. Connecticut Department of Education, "2012: The Year for Educational Reform," 2012.

48. Jacqueline Rabe Thomas, "New Accountability System Will Rank Every Public School," *Connecticut Mirror*, http://ctmirror.org/story/18337/new-system-will-rank-every-public-school-one-five-categories, November 30, 2012.

49. Kathy Megan, "Hartford Students in Regional Magnets and 'Open Choice' Outperform Kids in City Schools," *Hartford Courant*, October 25, 2012.

50. Kathy Megan, "Testing More Time in School," *Hartford Courant*, December 1, 2012, p. A1+.

51. Vanessa de la Torre, "Hartford to Receive $5 Million for Education," *Hartford Courant*, December 6, 2012, pp. A1 and A6.

52. For complete operating plan, see http://www.windham.k12.ct.us/downloads/about/WindhamThreeYearSOP-5-30-2012.pdf.

FIVE

Off the Streets and into Class

The Making of the Dual College Enrollment Program

Edward Osborn

> The biggest thing these kids need to know is that they matter.
> —Margaret Letterman, psychology professor

Throughout my professional career—from my days as an Upward Bound instructor in the early 1970s, an ESL coordinator, and a professor at Ramapo College of New Jersey to my years as an administrator in the City University of New York System and the University of Maine System—I have been committed to broadening educational access for minorities, low-income families, and other students whose life circumstances have made attending college an unlikely proposition.

When I embarked on my current appointment as president of Eastern Connecticut State University in 2006, I was not sure how I might continue my commitment to expanding educational access, but I was eager to explore the possibilities. As chapters 3 and 4 explain, during my first year at Eastern, I discovered that the challenges and struggles of Connecticut's Latino population mirrored some of my own experiences growing up in New Jersey as a newcomer from Puerto Rico.

I also was astonished to learn that the academic performance of Connecticut's low-income, urban, and Latino and African American students trailed that of their white, more affluent counterparts by the widest margins in the nation. I understood clearly the barriers and hurdles that these youth faced in achieving academic success and eventual college matriculation. I was resolved to do something—to find some form of positive intervention in the lives of Connecticut's inner-city students—in the face of the worst achievement gap in the United States.

By fall 2007, I was ready. My good friend and colleague Dr. Estela López, the vice chancellor for academic affairs for the Connecticut State University System at the time, had been in conversation with the staff at Hartford Public High School (HPHS) and arranged for me to visit their guidance counselors. Finding ways to get more Hartford students into and through college was on everyone's mind.

I was struck by the commitment of HPHS's Jeffrey Bartlett and Richard Serrano to improving the lives of their students, and we all quickly agreed that we needed to try new, innovative models if we wanted these young people to succeed at and graduate from college. Given my experiences growing up in Newark, New Jersey, as well as seeing the negative impact of inner-city life on students' motivation and the limited support systems around them, I believed that what we needed to do first was to get students out of their neighborhoods and onto our campus if we wanted them to be successful. Everything else in our model would support this basic concept—surround the students with a positive, safe, and supportive environment that would reinforce the learning and personal growth that could occur. The staff at HPHS liked the idea, and I promised to return with a plan of action after working with my staff. As I drove back to Willimantic that day, I felt energized yet fully aware that we had much work ahead to make our dream a reality.

—Elsa Núñez

The first steps in launching the Dual College Enrollment Program (DCEP) at Eastern were threefold: first, create and convene an internal team that would serve as the backbone of the program; second, develop partnerships with two key partners—HPHS and Quinebaug Valley Community College (QVCC); and third, conduct research into best practices and models that could be used to develop the program.

Dr. Núñez remembers the first meeting that she had with her staff to talk about creating and implementing the DCEP:

> In the room were Rhona Free, vice president for academic affairs; Kenneth DeLisa, vice president for institutional advancement; and Kimberly Crone, director of admissions at the time. I asked Dr. Free to begin developing a framework for the academic and support systems on campus that would be needed to accommodate a cohort of students from Hartford Public High School. I asked Mr. DeLisa to seek private funding that could provide essential financial support to DCEP students. And I asked Ms. Crone to research what special college programs might exist elsewhere to enroll and support inner-city students.

Eastern's administration also began identifying other staff to support the new program, including Indira Petoskey, then director of the Intercultural Center, who became the program's coordinator during its first four years and was a key to its early success. Over time, housing staff, counselors, advisers, admissions staff, and many others on campus have become formal or informal members of the DCEP team.

A PARTNERSHIP FROM DAY ONE

From the first day that Dr. Núñez visited Jeffrey Bartlett and Richard Serrano in the early fall of 2007, the staff and faculty at HPHS have been supportive and proactively involved in the DCEP. Whether encouraging students to work hard in preparation for interviewing for the program, determining which students were the best fit for the program, or inviting DCEP students to return to the high school to share their experiences at Eastern, HPHS administrators and faculty have demonstrated that they believe in the program and value its ability to transform the lives of the HPHS graduates who come to Eastern's campus. The HPHS team includes college specialist Jeff Bartlett, counselor Charlene Senteio, former and current principals of the high school's three academies, and other educators at the high school who believe in their students' potential.

The staff and faculty at QVCC—Bob Fernandez and Alfred Williams in the program's early years and now José Aponte—have also been supportive partners with Eastern's team in recruiting and serving DCEP students. Not only does QVCC provide academic instruction during the students' first year, but its faculty and staff have also been an integral part of the program's support systems, including providing financial aid, advising, and tutoring services. In addition to providing advice and counsel to DCEP students, an ongoing conversation between QVCC staff and the DCEP program coordinator at Eastern helps to identify issues and resolve them quickly. Daily communications and weekly reports also help to ensure that frontline staff at QVCC and Eastern share in the progress of DCEP students.

As students from Manchester High School have been added to the program, Manchester's guidance director David Stetson has also been involved as a member of the DCEP team.

DUE DILIGENCE

Eastern's DCEP project team spent much of the 2007–2008 school year researching dual enrollment programs and best practices around the country. The term *dual enrollment* has been used over the years to describe a number of educational options for students. Most of these programs are partnerships between high schools and colleges—community colleges or four-year institutions—in which high school students gain college credit or concurrent college/high school credits for taking college courses. In some cases, college instructors staff the courses at the high school, while in other situations, high school students visit the college campus to take the classes. One recent study concluded that 74 percent of dual enrollment courses are taught in the high schools.[1]

This dual or concurrent enrollment model has been around for decades and has principally focused on providing additional educational options for top-achieving students. As researchers Elisabeth Barnett of Teachers College at Columbia University and Liesa Stamm of Rutgers University conclude, providing high-performing high school students with early college options "continues to be the central purpose of dual enrollment nationally."[2] In fact, a study of New England dual enrollment initiatives in 2004–2005 found that while thirty-three of fifty-two responding high school districts had dual enrollment partnerships with a college or university, only three of the thirty-three allowed at-risk, lower-performing students to participate. Of the thirty-three colleges that responded to the survey (eleven community colleges and twenty-two senior institutions), nineteen participated in a dual enrollment partnership, but only three of those involved at-risk high school students.[3]

This research led Dr. Núñez and her team to several conclusions. First of all, dual enrollment programs, for the most part, were for high-achieving high school students, with course location being the variable. They did not involve a community college or university partnership such as the one that Eastern envisioned, nor were they aimed at low-income students who have finished high school. Second, while many of the dual enrollment models included coursework at a community college or four-year institution, they were not residential; the students still lived in their home neighborhoods. In addition to this aspect of dual enrollment programs, the same issue—living in inner-city neighborhoods—has been a factor in the lack of success of community college students from urban areas.

By their very nature, most community colleges are commuter schools. Inner-city students commuting to a community college, no matter how dedicated they are, must still deal with the pressures, challenges, and obstacles inherent in their home environments. Peer and family pressures, street violence, and other symbols of the poverty cycle make success difficult for community college students from city neighborhoods. For instance, only about 30 percent of disadvantaged minority students who attend a community college, predictably from city environments, graduate with an associate's degree within six years,[4] and only 11.6 percent of students who start at a community college earn a bachelor's degree within six years.[5]

These research data caused Eastern's administration to keep coming back to its initial premise—it needed to get students out of their home neighborhoods if they were going to be successful. The consensus was that having them conduct their academic studies in a supportive campus environment separate from the streets of the inner city could only increase their chances of success. This principle became the cornerstone of the DCEP program, which remains unique in its community college–university partnership and on-campus residential components.

THE MODEL THAT EASTERN DEVELOPED AND IMPLEMENTED

The key components of the DCEP model at Eastern are sixfold: take students out of their home neighborhoods, recruit students who are most likely to succeed, provide them with essential financial resources, make sure that they are academically ready, surround them with a strong support system, and promote a culture of inclusion on campus.

Take the students out of their home neighborhoods and house them on campus. In a September 2012 interview, former director of admissions Kimberly Crone, now at Southern Connecticut State University, recalls,

> From the beginning, Dr. Nuñez believed we needed to take the students out of the environment they had lived in for 18 years, and put them on our campus in a structured, supported environment to improve their chances of success. That meant getting them away from their home neighborhoods, with all the family commitments, full-time jobs after school, the street gangs, and the violence.

> Our early experiences in the program supported this fundamental premise. We had one student in the first cohort who had worked six hours a day in a grocery store each day after school, and was often too tired to do her homework. Another had a very sick parent and had to take care of her mother as well as her younger siblings. Another had experienced a shooting down the street the day before he came to our summer orientation. Some had language barriers.

> These kids were diamonds in the rough, had lights in their eyes, but lacked the family and other support they needed to move ahead. So our concept was to get them on our campus and surround them with positive influences.

Recruit students who can succeed in the program. When Dr. Núñez first presented Eastern's plan to Jeff Bartlett and his team at HPHS in spring 2008, they were pleased and excited. Jeff and his colleagues felt that they could find and recruit students who were on track to complete high school on time, in a city where many students do not finish high school at all. However, all the partners—HPHS counselors, Bob Fernandez and enrollment management director Alfred Williams at QVCC, and the staff at Eastern—were in agreement: they needed to find students who showed creativity, ambition, integrity, and a sense of personal responsibility despite adverse personal or family situations.

The first interview team visited HPHS in May 2008; since then, the program's partners have worked to start the screening and interviewing process sooner. Each spring, a team of five or six staff from Eastern and QVCC travel to HPHS (and now also Manchester High School and other high schools in the Hartford area) to conduct one-on-one interviews with approximately twenty students, three per staff person.

"We were less concerned about their academic records; the admissions office already had that documentation," explains Joe McGann, director of institutional advancement at Eastern, who joined the interviews beginning with the 2009 cohort. "It was a question of whether or not the student was mature enough to be a college student; were they ready to roll their sleeves up and do the work."

HPHS's Jeff Bartlett describes how the screening process has occurred over time:

> One thing I have done here is to make sure our guidance counselors and principals (we have three separate academies, each with a separate counselor and principal) are aware of and support the program. We want to be sure they understand the type of student we think can succeed.

> Before the Eastern admissions staff come to campus, we pull together a list of about 25–30 potential candidates for the program from the three academies. Eastern has also done a tremendous job of sending admissions staff to our high school to support the program, including interviewing candidates, conducting placement tests, and meeting with our staff and students.

In addition to Accuplacer English and math placement tests, students take the Learning and Studies Strategies Inventory self-assessment of motivation. Test scores and grades are also considered, but the key factors remain motivation and maturity.

Charlene Senteio is the only guidance counselor for the five hundred students in HPHS's Law and Government Academy:

> So I know all the kids. For this program, I look for "stick-to-it-ive-ness." By senior year, I know the students' progress and regression. I have seen them mature. A few have surprised me; by senior year, they have done a 180-degree turnaround. Selection is not a formal process. I identify possible candidates early on and then watch them during senior year. Some get into a school on their own or pursue a different direction. Sometimes I use the DCEP program as motivation: "I think you could do this Eastern program, but you need to show me something. Work harder." I also look to teachers for their recommendations—how do the students go about seeking help? Do they wait until the last minute?

Senteio also notes that adding a current DCEP student to the interview team that comes to Hartford—a strategy started for the fall 2011 cohort—is another important screening element: "They can tell immediately if someone is being honest about their goals or motivations."

Provide DCEP students with the financial resources they need to persist and succeed. Dr. Núñez and her colleagues realized immediately that DCEP students and their families were not in a position to afford a college education without help. To be eligible for financial aid, the students needed to complete the Federal Application for Financial Student Aid, a daunting task for families unfamiliar with the process, but Jeff Bartlett helped his HPHS students through the application.

For purposes of financial aid eligibility, DCEP students can be considered full-time at only one institution; since they take twelve credits at QVCC in their first semester, they are considered full-time students there. An agreement between the community colleges and state universities in Connecticut allowed the students to take one course at Eastern at no charge as matriculated students at QVCC. That left the issue of how to pay for housing and meals. While the students qualified for financial aid at QVCC, neither the community college nor the university could use public funds to pay for the students' room and board at Eastern during their first semester.

The university also realized that finding funds would be an ongoing task to help students pay for their tuition, room and board, books, and other costs once they became full-time students at Eastern. As future cohorts were added to the first group of students in 2008, the ability to help DCEP students manage their finances so that money would be neither a burden nor a barrier was a fundamental issue that Eastern would have to address on a continuing basis.

An initial request to the Hartford Foundation for Public Giving's Latino Endowment Fund resulted in a generous donation to provide early support for the program. Over time, funding has been received from eight other foundations, including more than $500,000 from the U.S. Department of Justice and the SBM Charitable Foundation, as well as from private donors. In 2013, the Hartford Foundation for Public Giving provided a second grant to the program in the amount of $269,200 to expand it to other Hartford high schools. Kenneth DeLisa and his staff in the Office of Institutional Advancement have continued their private philanthropy and federal grant-writing efforts so that all DCEP students in the pipeline can receive the financial support they need to stay in the program and succeed.

In addition to Pell Grants, Connecticut State University Grants, ECSU Foundation scholarships, subsidized loans, and other financial aid, each DCEP student is hired to work ten to twelve hours a week in an on-campus job. These jobs not only provide income but also give students opportunities to develop time management skills, self-discipline, and leadership skills.

Make sure that the students are academically ready. Most of the more than sixty students who have enrolled in the DCEP program have not met Eastern's traditional admissions requirements—grade point average, SAT scores, class rank—and some have had significant deficiencies in mathematics and language skills. While immersing these students in Eastern's social environment of residential life, student clubs, and campus activities has proved to be a positive change in their lives, expecting them to succeed immediately in class by taking a full load of fifteen university-level credits in the first semester would not have been unrealistic. Their academic skills needed to catch up to their life skills at the same time that they were adjusting to their new campus environment.

To prepare students for full-time coursework at Eastern, the university has worked with the staff at QVCC's Willimantic Center to enroll DCEP students in fundamental courses in reading, writing, mathematics, and other classes in their first semester while taking one class at Eastern as a group. Most students are then prepared to enroll full-time at Eastern by their second semester. Since QVCC's Willimantic location is only ten minutes down the hill from Eastern's dormitories, traveling between the two sites during the first semester has been seamless and convenient for DCEP students.

Surround the students with a comprehensive, proactive support system. The first element in Eastern's support system is a two-day summer orientation program, when DCEP students learn what it is like living and studying on a college campus, receive financial aid counseling, and get to know one another. The experience is eye-opening for all involved. Associate director of admissions Christopher Dorsey recounts picking up his first DCEP student in Hartford in July 2008 to take him back to campus for orientation:

> I knew it was a violent neighborhood, but I was still unprepared. The student told me there had been a shooting down the street the week before, and someone bleeding from a chest wound had walked by his house while he was sitting on the porch. He had trouble sleeping and told me nothing good was going to happen to him if he stayed there.

Some of Dorsey's stories are lighter:

> It's funny watching the students' cell phones lose their power bars as they head from Hartford toward rural Willimantic; they think they are leaving civilization as they know it. [Another student's mother] stared at her daughter as she walked away to go to orientation as if she would never see her again. I told the mother, "She'll be fine; we will take care of her." The daughter was very shy, but within two months, she was talkative and confident, and now she is a resident assistant. I saw a huge leap of maturity as she came out of her shell.

While the faculty and staff at Eastern understood from the outset that DCEP students needed close supervision and guidance, it was important not to create a separate support system for the program. The same academic and social issues facing DCEP students can be found in varying degrees across the entire student body. Personal issues, such as being homesick, relationship issues, and finances, as well as academic issues—what courses to take, difficulties with certain subjects, study habits—are common on any college campus and in all sectors of a student population. Fortunately, the DCEP program was launched at the same time as Eastern's 2008–2013 strategic plan, which included a major initiative to enhance Eastern's support systems for all students.

At the same time that the DCEP began in fall 2008, Eastern used funding from the Nellie Mae Education Foundation and a five-year, $1.5 million Title III grant from the U.S. Department of Education to create a one-stop Academic Services Center on the ground floor of the library. The center combines professional and peer tutoring in discipline-specific coursework, specialized math/writing assistance, academic advising, and other support services in one convenient location near other library resources. Each year, more than two thousand students visit the center, logging more than ten thousand visits a year. Eastern also hired more professional advisers and instituted a four-tiered advising model that includes preenrollment advising, first-year advising, advising toward one's major, and career counseling. In addition to making these services available to all Eastern students, the program provides one-on-one mentors for DCEP students.

Another element of Eastern's student success model is the extensive program of support that freshman students receive in the residence halls. Residence hall directors and resident assistants organize hall and floor socials; encourage freshmen to get involved with clubs and intramurals; conduct life skill workshops on time management, personal finance, and study habits; and plan programs to help students declare their major—all to assist freshmen in adapting to college in the first six weeks of school, the time when national data indicate that they are most susceptible to dropping out. A predictive model based on hard data has also been implemented so that at-risk students can be identified at the earliest possible time and appropriate interventions undertaken.

An unanticipated yet natural addition to the university's system of assistance for DCEP students is their peer support for one another. For example, "Nicole," a first-semester student in fall 2012, was told that her financial aid package at QVCC had been denied. The people at QVCC had even called her mother. She was crushed, and she thought that she had to pack her bags. Nicole's fellow students came to DCEP program coordinator Rick Hornung and asked him to intervene. With some investigation and a phone call, Nicole's financial aid problem was rectified. This culture of peer support extends across the entire student body at

Eastern, but DCEP students share some of the same backgrounds and on-campus issues and are especially sure to watch out for one another on a daily basis.

Promote a culture of inclusion and diversity on campus. In many urban communities across our country, including Hartford, Connecticut, most residents are Latino or African American. Students from these communities are not used to interacting or living with Caucasian students. Students from rural or suburban communities are often equally unfamiliar with the lives of Latinos, African Americans, and other minorities. For many Eastern students, living in the university's residence halls and going to classes with students from diverse backgrounds is the first time that they have experienced people from different cultures and ethnic heritages.

For DCEP students, it is an important learning opportunity. As Burr Hall director Luz Burgos explains, "even though the dual enrollment students share high school experiences and ethnic similarity, they seem to recognize the need to make friends outside of their own circle. Immersing themselves at Eastern is a growth process."

To support its campus commitment to diversity, Eastern presents an array of multicultural events on campus each year, coordinated by the Intercultural Center, individual academic departments, and other university offices. African dance, Mexican folk stories, lecturers from the United Kingdom, and visiting artists from Cuba are just a few examples of the more than 150 cultural events and guest visitors that came to campus this past year.

Perhaps the most significant factor in promoting a culture of inclusion and diversity on campus is Eastern's commitment to hiring minority faculty. A study of faculty at U.S. universities by the U.S. Department of Education indicated that Eastern has the largest percentage of minority faculty of all higher education institutions in Connecticut, including Yale, Wesleyan, and the University of Connecticut. Twenty-six percent of Eastern faculty members are minorities, compared to 16 percent at Yale and Central Connecticut State University, 15 percent at the University of Connecticut and Southern Connecticut State University, and 14 percent at Western Connecticut State University.[6] Not only does such diversity provide role models for minority students, but a diverse faculty also provides all Eastern students with a broader cultural and intellectual perspective.

OUTCOMES

Students experience many things in college—they meet new friends, learn social and citizenship skills, and practice their leadership—but their common goal is to graduate. This is the reason that Eastern Connecticut

State University exists, and it is the ultimate measure of the DCEP. Of fifty-one students recruited into the DCEP program in its first five years, twenty-three have graduated or are on track to graduate within six years. While this rate of 45 percent is somewhat lower than the university's overall six-year graduation rate, which has averaged 51 percent over the past three years and is the highest among Connecticut's four state universities, it is encouraging when taken in context with the backgrounds of the students enrolled. When one considers that the Hartford public school system has the lowest high school graduation and college enrollment rates of any urban area in New England, and that less than 5 percent of Hartford's high school class of 2003 was predicted to graduate from a four-year college by 2008,[7] the success of the DCEP is impressive. An additional fifteen of the project's recruits—29 percent—are studying at a community college or are enlisted in the military. One has transferred to a private college, and another is employed in a management position in a retail operation in Hartford.

Another interesting theme that has emerged from the program is its motivational impact on students who "stop out." As is the case with many college students, personal issues, finances, academics, and other factors have caused some DCEP students to drop out or be dismissed from the university. Two DCEP students who left due to poor academic performance and three who left for personal reasons subsequently enrolled in community college courses and/or straightened out other circumstances in their lives, recommitted themselves to their academics, and were then readmitted to Eastern in fall 2012.

As dean of students Walter Diaz explains,

> These stop outs are a success story. To have a student dismissed for academic reasons, go to a community college and then come back within a semester or summer demonstrates they are determined to be successful at Eastern. They mature tremendously in that short period of time. They tell me, "I am going to get it right. I am more focused; I know what I need to do." As we see their grades improve we can validate that they are going to class, doing their homework, going to their on-campus jobs. Giving these kids a second chance is an important component in this program.

An unexpected outcome of the program is the handful of Hartford and Manchester high school students interviewed each spring for the DCEP program who did not think that they were "college material" but qualified to enroll at Eastern through the university's normal admissions process. While they do not need the high-touch support of the DCEP, these students were not planning on going to college. As a result of the DCEP screening process, they still end up at Eastern.

Although not a direct measure of the success of the DCEP, a November 2012 study by the Education Trust, a national education advocacy group, gives the university further confidence that the systems that it has put into place to support the success of all students are working. In its report, the Education Trust announced that Eastern ranked number one in a national study of the improvement of six-year graduation rates of Latino students among public universities and colleges. For the class of full-time, first-time students entering in fall 1998, the six-year graduation rate was barely 20 percent for Latino students at Eastern. However, for those Latino students entering in 2004, the proportion who had graduated by 2010 was 57.8 percent, the largest improvement among the 228 public institutions in the study.[8] This is good news for all students at Eastern but especially for minority and economically disadvantaged students such as those enrolled in the DCEP.

Finally, independent of outcome measures are the success stories that occur each day on campus. One DCEP student became the president of his residence hall in his first year. One student ended up studying in Italy for a semester; another studied in London; and two went to Jamaica to work in the schools there over spring break 2011. Two May 2012 graduates are applying to graduate school, and a recent 2013 graduate is enrolled in a master's degree program at Providence College.

A significant number of DCEP students have blossomed to become student leaders, serving as officers of different student clubs and organizations or as activists and advocates in such on-campus departments as the Women's Center, the Intercultural Center, and the Center for Community Engagement. Two DCEP students shared their perspectives at a major student conference in New York City in fall 2012. And two DCEP students—Todd Aviles and Kayla Bynum—returned to HPHS on a regular basis to counsel and motivate the next cohort of dual college enrollment students.

The students in the DCEP have come from a range of backgrounds, yet all seek to take advantage of the same opportunity that has been put before them. Their stories range from the poignant to the tragic. Losing siblings to street shootings, family suicides, foster care, divorce, homelessness, abandonment by both parents—these true, personal stories reflect the violence, chaos, and instability of the neighborhoods from which DCEP students come.

To survive the violence of the streets of Hartford and Manchester and graduate from high school is already an accomplishment. To enter a new world at Eastern, away from home and familiar neighborhoods, and confront a new living situation, new social circles, and a new educational experience is an act of courage. From their circumstances, these students have found strength, and on Eastern's campus, they have found hope and direction. Drawing on their inner strength and the support around them, they are committed to persevere and succeed.

The following six chapters recount the personal stories—the challenges as well as the triumphs—of six DCEP students. These are stories of struggle, heartache, hope, and redemption. Some of these students have graduated from Eastern, while others are still enrolled in the program pursuing their degrees. In each instance, they are a reminder of what can be done when promise and potential are given the opportunity to grow. Each of these students demonstrates the transformative power of education and the value of saving lives, one at a time.

NOTES

1. Elisabeth Barnett, senior research associate, Teachers College, Columbia University, and Liesa Stamm, senior research associate at Rutgers University's Center for Children and Childhood Studies, "Dual Enrollment: A Strategy for Educational Advancement of All Students," Blackboard Institute, June 2010, p. 3.

2. Barnett and Stamm, "Dual Enrollment," p. 2.

3. Nancy Hoffman and Amy Robins, "Headstart on College: Dual Enrollment Strategies in New England, 2004–05," Jobs for the Future, June 2005.

4. Michael Danziger, "An Independent Path to College Success," *Connections*, spring 2007, p. 19.

5. Kevin Carey, "U.S. College Graduation Rate Stays Pretty Much the Same," The Quick and the Ed, http://www.quickanded.com, December 2, 2010; citing National Center for Education Statistics's Beginning Postsecondary Survey.

6. U.S. Department of Education's Integrated Postsecondary Education Data System, reported in *The Chronicle of Higher Education*, http://chronicle.com/section/Faculty-Data/133, September 30, 2011. More than 3,800 two- and four-year colleges and universities from all fifty states were analyzed.

7. Danziger, "An Independent Path."

8. The Education Trust, "Advancing to Completion: Increasing Degree Attainment by Improving Graduation Rates and Closing Gaps for Hispanic Students," September 20, 2012.

III

Student Stories

SIX

Federica Bucca, Class of 2013

Thank you, Mami, for teaching me the importance of helping others!

SEPTEMBER 11, 2001

I was born in Mendoza, Argentina, the oldest of three children. My mother's name is Andrea Arce, and my father's name is José Bucca. My oldest brother is also José Bucca; my youngest brother is named Italo Bucca.

My mother's aunt Maria Del Rosario and her family moved to the United States in the 1980s, and she was always telling my mom and dad that we should follow them. Maria would say, "Andrea, there are a lot of opportunities here in the United States. They are hiring, there are a lot of jobs, the education is better here for your kids, and maybe José will change his ways."

My father had some bad habits—drugs and drinking. My mom knew that if we stayed in Argentina and my dad kept up his habits, we wouldn't have a future.

Eventually, my parents decided to come to America. My dad came to the states in 2000 to get settled and find a job, and my mom, my two younger brothers, and I were to come after he was ready. He ended up in New Jersey, near my mother's aunt and her family.

The day that we were to move was finally settled on—September 11, 2001. We were going to fly into JFK airport in New York. I can't remember what happened, but my dad called a few days before and said that things weren't quite ready for us in New Jersey and we would have to wait another month. We traveled to the United States exactly a month later—on October 11.

71

I was nine years old and lived five thousand miles from New York, so it was only when we finally got here that I really understood what had happened on September 11. My dad explained to me that a major terrorist attack on the United States had occurred that day, with New York City at the center of it. We would never have been able to land at JFK that day. It would have been very strange getting here on September 11; I am sure that we would have been diverted elsewhere—our first day in the United States, if we had even made it this far, would have been crazy.

When we arrived on October 11, the airport was swarming with armed men and guard dogs, and there were barriers everywhere. I remember the metal detectors and being patted down. Being new to the United States and not being able to speak English was difficult enough, but I could also feel the tension in the air, and all the security frightened me.

The people of New York were having a difficult time recovering from the attack, but I was too young to understand their pain and suffering. All I remember is that I was sad that I wasn't going to get to see the Twin Towers. When I had looked up New York City on the Internet back home in Argentina, the Twin Towers was one of the pictures that I had seen.

We came on a Wednesday and stayed the night at my Aunt Alejandra Quintero's house. The next day, my father took my mother, me, and my brothers into Manhattan to see the sights. We went to McDonald's, and I remember being amazed by the plasma TV screens—I had never seen televisions like that before! My brothers and I were super excited to see Manhattan and to be in what was basically a new world for us.

FRIDAY THE 13TH

On Friday, two days after we arrived, my parents apparently had an argument. I later learned my father was still drinking and abusing drugs. He got a ride to the airport, told the authorities that he was an Argentinian immigrant who did not want to be in the United States any longer, and they let him leave. His ninety-day visa had run out months before, so he was here illegally. He was literally banished from this country for ten years. More important, he had abandoned my mother only two days after she had arrived in the United States.

There she was—two days off an airplane from another country so different from the United States, left by her husband to take care of three young children by herself, without a job, and not knowing a word of English. I was only nine, José was seven, and Italo was five. I could feel how depressed, lonely, and desperate my mother was, but I was not in a position to be of much help.

I have never totally forgiven my father for abandoning us almost as soon as we had arrived in the states, but I understand what frustrations he felt. Mendoza is a city in northwest Argentina about sixty miles from the Chilean border. The city has about a hundred thousand people, maybe a little more, but with all the suburbs around it, there are probably almost a million people in the metropolitan area. We lived in the city, and my father rented and ran a parking lot in downtown Mendoza that was used by doctors, lawyers, and other wealthy professionals to park their cars. He had started working there as an attendant when he was a teenager, and his three younger brothers had worked there too. When the man who owned the lot decided to sell it, my dad took it over. We weren't rich, but we had enough money to own a nice house. My dad worked Monday through Friday at the parking lot and was his own boss; he had a hired worker for the weekends.

When my father got to New Jersey, it was like starting over at the bottom. He came on a ninety-day visa and ended up working the third shift, seven days a week. He didn't like having to answer to someone, because he had been his own boss for years. He had some bad habits in Argentina, and he was still using drugs when we got here in 2001. But whatever problems he was dealing with, he still shouldn't have left my mom all alone.

We really couldn't stay forever with my cousins in New Jersey. My mother's sister Mariana (who was also my godmother), her husband, and their two children lived in Hartford, Connecticut, and she encouraged my mom to move to Hartford to live with them until we could get on our feet. A month after we arrived in New Jersey, we came to Connecticut and moved in with my aunt and her family. She was working at El Mercado—a supermarket five houses down the street from her apartment—and they needed a cashier. She told them about my mother, and my mom started work there. Even then, I remember how I would show up at the store after school to bag groceries and would make $10 to $25 in tips. I have always worked for my money. Within a year, Mariana and her family moved to North Carolina, and my mother, my brothers, and I had their old apartment to ourselves.

CULTURE SHOCK

When we arrived in Hartford, there were certainly many other people there from Latin America. But what many people don't understand is that each nation is very different. Argentinians, Cubans, Puerto Ricans, Mexicans—we all speak Spanish, but each country has its own culture, its own traditions. I was meeting all these people who talked differently from me. Even other Latinos who spoke Spanish had a different accent than I had.

My father is Sicilian and Argentinian, but my mom's parents were both from Argentina, and most of the people in Mendoza look alike. I was from a country where everyone talked the same, ate the same food, and pretty much had the same taste in music—the same tastes in many things. In Hartford, I was trying new foods that I had never tried before, and I was learning terms in Spanish that I had never used before.

I also had never seen a black person in Argentina. It wasn't until I arrived in the United States that I saw someone of African descent. I realized that I had been living in a bubble—an Argentinian bubble. In this new country, I was presented with a lot of different bubbles, and I got the chance to poke at them to learn from each bubble. In a way, I was not just coming to a new country; I was looking at a mirror of the entire world for the first time.

I like the diversity in America. It's one of my favorite things about the United States. Even within the Latin American community, you might have ten Puerto Ricans, ten Dominicans, and five Mexicans, but they might all be different because they might all come from different regions in their own countries. Even within their own bubbles, they are learning something new from one another. I like that.

Every day, I was experiencing new things. For instance, my family never ate rice and beans until we got to Hartford. In Argentina, we ate a lot of *asado*, which is grilled meat, steak, and *morzillas*—blood sausages. We ate soups and pasta, and we made a potato salad that is different from how it is made here. In Hartford, through the Puerto Rican families in the neighborhood, we discovered plantains and pork chops. At first I said to my mother, "What is this stuff? I want real food." But we soon experienced American pizza and other new foods, and I realized that I could hold on to my heritage and still try new things.

School was also very different in Hartford than it had been in Mendoza. Our school there was divided into two shifts, and I went to school from 8:00 a.m. to 12:30 in the afternoon. We had uniforms in elementary school—a little white apron, a skirt, and black shoes. The boys had blue doctor's aprons and black shoes. Every morning, we would line up outside and say the Argentinian pledge of allegiance as the flag was raised. It was strange to move to Hartford and recite the American pledge of allegiance inside our classrooms as it was played over the intercom. I also discovered that even though I had to learn the English language, I had already learned many of the lessons that were being taught here. Even in the seventh and eighth grades, I seemed to already know half of what was being taught. Maybe that is the reason why I was getting good grades.

Another difference from Mendoza to Hartford was safety in the neighborhood. In Argentina, I would play outside with my friends each afternoon—I think I knew everyone in my neighborhood. When we got to Hartford, my mom didn't feel that it was safe for us to play outside unless she was watching us on her days off. It wasn't just my family; I think all of the kids in the neighborhood were afraid of the streets.

We also had to get used to the weather. In Argentina, we had all four seasons but no snow where we lived. I didn't see snow until we got to Hartford, and south of the equator, winter is from May to September. My birthday is on December 30, and we always celebrated it in Argentina with an ice cream cake and a pool party in the summer. Christmas was a time for fireworks and outdoor festivities. Now the holiday season is all about hot cocoa, and all the parties are inside. The seasons are upside down!

I WILL EAT YOU

Without my father to support us and with facing a new culture and school where I had to learn a new language, I was pushed to grow up faster than I wanted. One thing that I knew how to do was to work hard in school, and I realized that doing well there and getting good grades was one way that I could help my mother.

I started school at Dominic F. Burns Elementary School on Putnam Street in the Frog Hollow neighborhood in Hartford. Even though I knew much of what was being taught in school, not knowing English meant that I was basically starting over. In fact, even though I had finished the fifth grade in Argentina, the school held me back, and I had to take the entire fifth grade over. It put me in the bilingual program "Spanish for All," and I started at the "0.0" level. You progressed through the levels— 1.1, 1.2, 2.1, 2.2, and so on. When I finished fifth grade, I was at the 3.2 level. I had two classmates who were jealous of me because I was catching up so quickly. They would bully me and my cousin Emiliano. As if that wasn't enough, they actually told their parents that I was bullying them! It was such a lie. One morning, as one of their fathers was dropping one of them off, he came up to me and said, "If you bother my daughter again, I will eat you."

Of course, the man didn't intend to eat me—he was simply trying to scare me, and he succeeded. I was frightened to death, so I told my teacher. She told the police, and the two kids who had been bullying me were suspended. But my mother was concerned for me and transferred me to another school, Maria Sanchez Elementary School, which was next to the El Mercado grocery store where she worked.

A DREAM SNATCHED FROM MY HANDS

At Sanchez Elementary School, I entered sixth grade and had my first male teacher, Mr. Torres. He was an amazing person. He believed in me. He went out of his way to explain things to me. He really cared about me, and I got a 4.0 grade point average in my bilingual classes. There was also a man who volunteered in Mr. Torres's class—John Hunt—who had a huge impact on my life. Mr. Hunt apparently was very wealthy. I later found out that he was a retired vice president from Travelers Insurance, but I didn't know that at the time; I just knew that he liked helping kids out in school. He would help kids who needed glasses by paying for them. He would help students with their assignments after school. He also had a scholarship program for kids in elementary school who he thought would continue to progress academically. He would recruit them in elementary school, tutor them, and follow them as they moved on to high school. They would get John Hunt Scholar awards to go on to college at the end of the program. I was getting all A's by this time, and he recruited me.

Mr. Hunt understood that I was still working on overcoming the language barrier, but he told me that students who kept up their grades could get scholarships to schools like the University of Connecticut, the University of Hartford, and St. Joseph's College in Hartford. He tutored me for several years, following me through Quirk Middle School and then on to Hartford Public High School. Sometimes he would call me on the phone and give me encouragement. He also would come to my middle school to stay in touch. When I got to ninth grade in Hartford Public High School, he continued to drop by to check in with me.

Then Mr. Hunt passed away when I was in tenth grade. Unfortunately, he had left no written documentation that I was one of the students under his wings who would ultimately receive one of his scholarships. Eventually, a woman took over Mr. Hunt's scholarship program. Some of the kids who had been recruited with me in elementary school and were now with me at Hartford Public High School continued to be involved, but when the woman came to our school, she left me alone. I was confused. "What's going on?" I thought. "Aren't I still in the program?" I asked her what the issue was, and that is when my world fell apart.

The woman explained to me that she could not help me, because I was "illegal." All the time that we had been in the United States, my mother, my brothers, and I had been undocumented—illegal aliens. My mother had been working under the table all the time that she had been at El Mercado. Now, she has her legal residency, pays taxes, and is working toward her American citizenship. But four years ago, when I was a senior in high school, the entire household was still undocumented.

HELPING MY MOM

Even though I wasn't here legally, I felt discriminated against. I had worked so hard for so long and not just in school. In sixth grade, I had made friends with Maria del Mar Casanova, a Dominican girl whose parents owned a restaurant—the Bean Pot. Maria used to help her parents on Saturdays at the Bean Pot, and I would go and hang out with her while she worked. Little by little, her parents got to know me, and they would say, "Federica, can you clean this table?" I was fine with helping out, since I was just sitting there, and then Maria would ask me, "Can you go bring that juice over to that customer?" Sure, I could do that; I thought of it as helping out my friend's family.

After a while, they started giving me $25 every Saturday. I was there from nine or ten in the morning until two in the afternoon, and they would give me $25 for the day. This was seventh grade and eighth grade, and when I got to high school, they hired me for good. Maria and I would come in every Saturday from five in morning—because it was a breakfast place—until two in the afternoon, and we would get $120 for the day. We were really working hard for the money, and it felt great. In the summer, I worked Monday through Saturdays—from eight to two on the weekdays and from five to two on Saturdays—all the way through high school until I graduated and came to Eastern. I will never forget the Casanova family for all the help they provided!

Part of the reason why I started working was to help my mother so that she didn't have to pay for my things anymore. I didn't want her to buy my clothes and other things; it was a little way for me to help her so that she could spend her money on other expenses.

I also have always felt that it was important to help others, and I started volunteering after school at Sanchez Elementary School, where I had attended the sixth grade, to help the younger kids with their homework.

I was working hard to help at home, and I had been working hard at school. Now, as I finished my junior year in high school, the dream that I had of going to college had disappeared. By the start of my senior year, everyone else was thinking about applying to college. A friend of mine was accepted early at Boston College on an athletic scholarship. Me? I was being told that I wouldn't be able to go to college. I was very discouraged and depressed. I started getting poor grades and had to drop a class that I was failing. This entire time, I'd been getting high honors, medals, and certificates for having good grades. Now here I was in my senior year, and people were telling me that I couldn't go to school. I was still an illegal alien—what was I to do?

ANOTHER DOOR OPENS

Throughout my senior year at Hartford Public High School, I fought my emotions. I had worked so hard for so long, and now where was I? I had been naïve for years, thinking that as long as I worked hard, I would be able to go to college and get a professional job, even though I wasn't a legal resident. Now I realized that without papers, I couldn't get a job, couldn't go to college, couldn't do anything. I was determined that I was not going to be working every Saturday for the rest of my life. I didn't want to be another statistic, another immigrant working for minimum wage. I started doing my own research, and my teachers helped me out, suggesting that I could go to a community college and pay for it with loans and my job.

At some point, my mother got hold of my father. He had finally returned to the United States from Argentina and was living and working in New Jersey. My parents had been divorced for some time, and he had gotten remarried.

About a month before my high school graduation, my father called to tell me he was in New Jersey. I still held a grudge against him for leaving us, and I really didn't want to talk with him. He explained to me that he had cleaned up, was working as a shuttle bus driver, and had gotten his papers—he was a legal resident. He had also petitioned the government to grant me residency as well, and we set up an appointment for me to see the immigration people in Hartford.

I called the lady who ran the Hunt Scholarship Program to tell her that I was about to be a legal resident, hoping that I could still get into college and receive a scholarship. She told me it was too late; everyone had already applied to colleges, and the money was all committed.

But I guess the people at Hartford Public High School still had faith in me. My guidance counselor told me about a program at Eastern Connecticut State University where I would take some courses at the local community college, live at Eastern, and eventually become a full-time student. The coordinator of the program came to our high school and interviewed me. She wanted to know why I felt that they should pick me. I explained that I had been working since I was eleven, volunteered in my old elementary school, was the captain of the cheerleading team, was in the Law and Government Academy at Hartford Public High School because I wanted to help people, and had been a good student most of my school years. I also had to explain that I was still an undocumented alien; I wasn't sure how my residency hearing would turn out. About two weeks after my interview, I was told that I was an alternate for the Dual College Enrollment Program, so I was still in limbo.

GOOD NEWS TIMES TWO

Then the darkness began to lift. A week after I learned that I was only an alternate for Eastern's program, I had my residency appointment. On May 5, 2009, I went to the federal court in Hartford and was interviewed. The lady across the table from me said, "It says here that you have Italian citizenship and Argentinian citizenship, so why do you want to be an American citizen?" I explained that I wanted to be legal in this country so that I could go to college and help my mom.

The lady said, "Okay," and signed my papers. It was over in ten seconds. I couldn't believe it! I started crying; it felt so good. My mom was waiting for me outside, and when I came out crying with a big smile on my face, she knew what had happened. It was a great moment.

Two hours later, my family—mom, José, Italo, and I—were going to a restaurant to celebrate the fact I was legal when my cell phone rang. It was my psychology teacher, Ms. Allison. She said, "Federica, I have great news." I stopped her and said, "Wait, I have good news too. I was about to call you." She asked me what news I had to share, and I told her that I had just received my residency papers, with an identification number in case I got accepted at Eastern. She said, "You're going to need it because the dual enrollment program people just called and said you had been accepted. You're going to Eastern."

On the same day, I had received the two pieces of news that I had been hoping for—I was now a legal resident, and I was going to college. It was so special to celebrate that day with my family. May 5, 2009, is a date that I will never forget.

Graduation day came a month later, and that was special too. My mother had asked my father to come to my high school graduation, but she didn't tell me. When I saw him there, I cried. On the one hand, I was still angry at him for what he had done so many years ago. On the other hand, I was happy to see him. My life was starting to come together.

DISCOVERING MYSELF

This is my senior year here at Eastern, and looking back, I am just very, very thankful to have had this opportunity; it has really changed my life. I have grown so much as a person. I have always been told that I'm a leader, but I never really applied my leadership skills until I got here. I have learned to live on my own, decide what I want to study, and figure out what classes I need to take. No one is telling me what to eat; no one is telling me that I need to get some rest or I'm going to get sick. And I know what I want to do with my life. I feel blessed.

One of the great things about Eastern is that it allows you so many opportunities to find yourself and then practice being yourself. That probably sounds strange, but it's true. In my case, I have been able to use my time in student clubs and my work as a volunteer to reinforce what I am learning in my major.

I decided to major in sociology in my sophomore year. I am also minoring in Spanish and anthropology. I noticed that I like to understand human behavior and how people act. I need to understand people to help them. After I graduate, I want to get my master's degree in social work or anthropology so that I can apply my knowledge and experience to help people.

I've had so many wonderful teachers. Nicholas Simon, a part-time lecturer in sociology, has also been great. Ever since I took his class Race and Ethnic Relations, he has kept an interest in me because I'm a first-generation college student—his research field of interest. He is working on his doctorate at the University of Connecticut. I volunteered to be interviewed for his research, and when we talked the other day, he couldn't stop telling me that I need to go to graduate school. He said that if I needed anything to let him know. So many of the faculty and staff at Eastern are like that; they are always there to help. I don't need to talk to them every day, but I always know they are there if I need something.

Another person who has really seen the good in me when I wasn't always at my best has been Walter Diaz, the dean of students. If I don't know how to do something, he suggests whom I should talk to, or he guides me to think through how to solve an issue.

Anthropology professor Ricardo Perez is someone else who has really helped me understand what it means to be from a Latin American country. He coordinates the Latin American Studies program and has helped me realize the importance of maintaining my heritage.

I meet students all the time whose parents or grandparents came from a Latin American country, but they never learned to speak Spanish and know nothing about their culture. They have been Americanized. Some of them want to get their Latino heritage back, but it's really hard for them because as you grow up, it's a lot harder to learn a new language and find your roots. Others completely disregard their family's past; it's as if they are saying, "That life was my parents' life, and this is mine."

I still have my customs with me, and I still apply them to my everyday life and to the kids I mentor. I have been in this country eleven years now, but I still maintain my culture, although I have yet to meet another Argentinian here at Eastern. I think that I can embrace the life I have here in the United States and still respect and maintain my family's traditions.

THE COMMUNITY IS MY CLASSROOM

As I have grown intellectually in my field of study, I have had a number of opportunities to use my academic skills on campus and in the community. For instance, I have been involved with the Organization of Latin American Students since I was a freshman. I was secretary of the club during my sophomore year, and we have done some great things as a club. We have been to conferences; we have gone to museums in New York City that focus on Latin American culture. We have done fun things on campus too—indoor skydiving, playing paintball, fun things that a lot of people don't get to do.

How do you skydive indoors? They set up a big room with four huge fans on the floor. You put on a suit and goggles, and when you step into the room, the fans blow you up into the air. There's a staff person with you so that you don't slam into the walls; you also have to learn how to float, but it was fun. I enjoyed it, and now I want to go skydiving for real.

The Organization of Latin American Students (OLAS) has also helped me make friends. When I was a freshman, Amelinda Vasquez was the vice president of the club. She graduated and went to graduate school, and she has returned to Eastern to be a residence hall director. She has really helped me get ready to be a resident assistant, which is my job on campus this year.

I also had a roommate in my freshman year—Taniah—who really didn't want to get involved. She is very shy, but I kept her by my side. In Burr Hall, we were known as "Rob and Big," but I call her "T." I told her, "T, you and I are going to be club officers in OLAS next year. I want those free sweaters." It was my way of giving her an incentive to go for it. I ended up being elected secretary, and she became the public relations officer. To this day, she thanks me because she realizes that it was a good experience.

Another program on campus that has really helped me is the Pathways to Leadership program. It gives club officers and other students a structured program to develop their leadership skills. Every student in the program gets to pick a mentor from a list of faculty and staff. When I saw President Núñez's name on the list, I couldn't believe it. But I figured, "What do I have to lose?" So I made an appointment through her secretary. When I went to see Dr. Núñez, I told her that she was pretty much the main reason why I was at Eastern, and I would be honored for her to be my mentor. That was all it took! I met with her once a week in the morning. We would talk about her experiences growing up, and she would ask me about my life and about my mom, about how school is going. She also wrote a recommendation that helped me get into ASPIRA, which is a middle school mentoring program funded through AmeriCorps. It was a great experience to get to know the president personally—how many college students get to say that?

The ASPIRA Association is the only national organization dedicated exclusively to helping develop the academic and leadership skills of Hispanic youth. It has been around since 1961, and it helps Puerto Ricans, Mexicans, African Americans, and non-Hispanic whites as well.

I CAN DO IT—YOU CAN DO IT

The ASPIRA program was just the first opportunity that I had to work in the Willimantic community. Knowing how many kids in town are also from Latino families has made volunteering in the community even more meaningful for me. It also fit in well with my on-campus job in the Center for Community Engagement. I ended up working with fifth- to eighth-grade students at Windham Middle School, tutoring during and after school. As one of the site coordinators, I helped recruit volunteers and mentors to tutor the kids in different subjects, such as English literacy, math, social studies, and science.

On Mondays and Wednesdays, I'll go to the middle school to mentor and tutor students there, but on Tuesdays and Thursdays, I'll go to the high school and keep up with the eighth graders who graduated from the middle school. I also work in the after-school program at Sweeney Elementary School in Willimantic. This past summer, I worked in the Bridges to the Future program. Rosie Hernandez, the woman who started the program, was my supervisor in the ASPIRA program. Now the Bridges program has been extended to the school year as an after-school program. We tell the kids that they need to get good grades and need to learn English because for most of them, Spanish is their native language. We also tell them not to forget where they come from. It's alright if your friend is white, black, or Chinese, and you're Hispanic. That's fine. That's America. We are a melting pot, so I take time to explain what that means. And I tell them that if I can go to college, so can they.

When I started volunteering, I realized that these students needed positive role models that they could relate to on a daily basis. The students see themselves in me, and the teaching goes both ways. While working with these kids, I have learned a lot about myself. I have gained confidence. I know what I want to do with my life.

I recently went to the Intercultural Horizons Conference in New York City to give a presentation on my experiences as a volunteer in a multicultural community. I explained how my work in Windham schools has helped guide me toward a career in the social services field.

I have come a long way since we left Mendoza. I have been fortunate, and people have supported me in so many ways. Helping others will be my way of giving back. Thank you, Mami, for teaching me the importance of helping others!

* * *

A case manager at the Village for Children and Families in Hartford, Connecticut, Federica started her master's program in education and counseling at Providence College in January 2014 and is also a resident hall director.

SEVEN

Ismael Gracia

I'm more than just the streets that I grew up on.

ALWAYS STARTING OVER

I am originally from Grand Rapids, Michigan, the youngest of five children. My father was born in Puerto Rico, and my mother came from Texas.

We didn't have a lot of money then, but we had enough to get by. All I needed was what my parents provided—love and a place to live. I had two older brothers whom I could always talk to and be around. They taught me a lot as I was growing up. We lived in a house in a nice neighborhood, and my uncle and his family lived just up the street. My mother also had a close friend there, so it wasn't too bad in my early childhood. The only thing is that we didn't always have enough money to get by. Things could be a little hard, but our family up the street always helped us out.

We moved to San Antonio, Texas, when I was four—in the middle of preschool—to be near my mother's parents. My grandparents lived across the street from us, and the elementary school was right up the street. But it was hard for me because I had made a lot of friends in Michigan. Moving to San Antonio was like starting all over. It was a new environment, a very different culture, and a drastically different climate from Michigan.

Once we moved from Michigan to Texas, the financial situation was also a lot harder. My brothers, sisters, and I didn't receive a lot of Christmas presents, because my parents were always trying to pay the bills. Sometimes we wouldn't have hot water to take a shower, the electricity would get cut off, or the gas for the stove would get shut off. Life started changing.

Having my grandparents there to support us and help us as much as possible made it manageable, but at the same time, you could see the struggle that my mother and my father were going through. They tried to make it seem as if everything was all right, and they told us that we didn't have to worry about anything. But kids are pretty perceptive.

My father did a lot of things for work. He worked in construction; he fixed cars—he did whatever he could find. Then we moved again—to Hartford—when I was six. My father's mother hadn't seen my dad in a while, so she came up with a big story that she was dying and needed to see him before she passed away. A week or two after he got that phone call, he said that we were moving again. It was hard on all of us. We had established a new place to live, somewhere that we thought was going to be permanent. I had made a lot of friends, and I was a good student in the first grade. The people in Texas also were very friendly; I remember that the man who lived next door would invite our whole family over to his house for barbeque, even though he didn't have any kids of his own.

When we got to Hartford, it was a shock. We went from living in a house to living in a small apartment that had to fit seven of us—my two sisters, my two brothers, me, and my parents. And the neighborhood was different—the streets seemed dirty, and it was more like the inner city than the neighborhood where we lived in San Antonio. I was uncomfortable from the beginning.

THE STRUGGLE TO SURVIVE

Within the first two or three months, we were already struggling. The apartment building that we were living in was on top of a restaurant that would catch on fire at night. It seemed like the building was always burning, so we always had to leave. We spent a lot of time in different hotels while the owners fixed up the restaurant downstairs. They put us up in cheap hotels—we had to bring our own curtains; the doors wouldn't lock; and the hallways smelled like urine and beer.

It was hard. I wasn't comfortable, and I didn't want to be in school in Hartford. I didn't know anyone, and it seemed like the people were not as friendly as the people had been in Texas or Michigan. It felt like a matter of survival. Even at my age, it was like an "every dog has to eat" mentality, so even as a young kid, I was getting in trouble. By third and fourth grade, I was getting into fights and starting to develop that mindset.

It was hard for me to go to school happy, seeing my parents struggle. I got suspended for the first time in the fourth grade for fighting. By then, I was just doing what I had to do to get by. In elementary school, sometimes they will pass you with a D just to avoid keeping you back. That's what I was settling for—as long as I didn't get an F, that's all I cared about. My parents tried to discipline me and tell me to do better, but it just went in one ear and out the other.

My focus was trying to help my parents financially. Even as a nine-year-old kid, I was thinking, "I can sell some baseball cards" or "I can fix some bikes up for my friends" to try to get some money to help my parents, because I didn't like to see them struggle.

TRYING TO FIND MY WAY

In fifth grade, my school started a basketball team. I really wanted to play, but I was told that I had to get my grades up. If I did that, I realized that I could play basketball and make new friends, so I started getting A's and B's, and I played basketball in fifth and sixth grade. It was fun. I made a lot of friends, started to get recognized by other kids in school, and was getting invited to sit at other people's lunch tables.

Middle school came along, and I started to hang with the wrong people. We would skip school, cheat on tests, get into fights . . . it was like we were getting in trouble on purpose so that people would see us as the tough guys in school. My parents weren't okay with it, because they knew that I could do better.

In the eighth grade, my grades were terrible—two F's, a D in science, a couple of C minuses—and I thought that maybe I could slide by and graduate with a D. Then I was told that I probably wasn't going to graduate. I started picking my grades back up, and I finished English with a B minus, got a C plus in science, a B in math, and an A in history. Despite all the trouble I had been in, I knew that I could succeed when I tried.

When I got to high school, I knew that I could be a better student, but I still had a lot of problems. It wasn't always my fault. My older brother had gone to Bulkeley High School with me, and he had a lot of trouble as well. Some of the people that he had fought with figured that they could pick on me once my brother was gone. I moved on to Hartford Public High School after ninth grade, and it was the same situation there.

My parents were also arguing a lot. My freshman year was tough. With all the negative stuff in school, to come home and see my parents arguing was difficult. Sometimes neither of my parents was there. They would show up at supper time, and I knew that they had already had a big fight. And our financial struggles were back. The rent would be late, or I'd go home and try to watch TV, but the cable was off because we couldn't afford to pay the cable bill.

I would go on jobs with my father—carpentry projects or fixing someone's car. He knew that I needed money in my pocket, so he would ask me to do side jobs with him. I was working on my own as well, so I was trying to help out with the bills.

OUR FAMILY IS CHANGED FOREVER

By my senior year, I was doing a lot of community service at an elementary school tutoring the kids. It was called Moylan Masterminds, a program at Moylan Elementary School that was sponsored by the Hartford Public Library. I had volunteered in my freshman and sophomore years and then was hired for the after-school program for first through sixth graders. We worked in teams, and I worked with my sister. We would help the kids get their homework done, and then they would have free time to do artwork, athletics, or something recreational. We wanted them to know that they had someone who was there to support them, someone to look up to. "This is the best time of our day. You even make homework fun," they would tell us. To see them smile and know that we were the reason—that was special. Their parents would even come up and thank us for helping their children.

I felt good. Then one day in October of my senior year, my family changed forever. The year before, when I was a junior, my mother and father had split up. I wanted to go with my father, but he told me to stay with my mother because he wasn't sure where he was going to live and my oldest sister wanted to live with him. She and my father were always the closest because she was the oldest. He had other children in Puerto Rico, but she was his first child with my mother. She was always his baby. So he took her with him. They were staying at my grandmother's and then ended up moving into a little apartment.

They got into a huge fight, and she left for three days. When my father didn't hear from my sister, he went off and destroyed a lot of their belongings. My sister went back to the apartment, and when she saw the computer smashed, the TV destroyed, and the holes punched in the walls, she came back to live with my mother. About a month later, my father called, said that he wanted to make up, and asked if she would like to go shopping. She asked if she could bring Kiki, my other sister's daughter, but my father said no. That was strange because he loved that little girl. It caught my sister off guard when he said, "No. I just want it to be a 'me and you' day. We can go shopping."

Later that day, I was at a friend's house when I got a phone call from my mother. She said that my father was in the hospital and my sister was dead. I left my friend's house running.

My father had taken my sister shopping, then drove on a back road, parked the car, and shot her. Then he shot himself. My sister died instantly. My father was in a coma, and about ten minutes after I got to the hospital, the doctor came out and told us that he was brain-dead. We could leave him on the machine or just pull the plug. We lost two loved ones on the same day.

Although the pain in my heart from what my father did that day will never leave me, my father was not a bad person. He was the best of people; he just made the wrong decision. He showed me how to mature as a man, how to do things the right way. I will always miss him and my oldest sister.

My senior year in high school changed immediately. I wasn't going to class. I wasn't going to work. I wasn't doing anything. I would just sit in my room all day. My grades started to slip. With all that happening and my mother already struggling to pay bills, we had to find money that we didn't have so that we could give my sister and my father a proper burial. I sold drugs to make money and collected money from friends and strangers, and we managed to bury my father and sister properly. There was a period of a month where we didn't have hot water. It was embarrassing to call my best friend and ask if I could come to his house to take a shower.

School was hard. I passed my classes with good grades but only because I had understanding teachers. By then, I just wanted to finish high school. I figured that I might take a year off and then probably go to Capital Community College in Hartford. That was my original plan. My oldest sister had gone to Capital and had been studying to be a teacher before she passed away.

I thought that I would work near my house, not have to travel very far, and go to Capital. I would stay in my neighborhood and be with the friends that I had there to support me. I didn't even apply to any colleges. I knew that when you attend a university, financial aid doesn't cover it all. With our money struggles, the thought of borrowing money and paying back college loans scared me. I always knew that once you finish college, you have to find a job; the loans aren't going to wait, and the interest keeps adding up. That's what scared me from applying to any universities or colleges. At Capital, there would be enough financial aid for me to make it.

A DOOR OPENS

At some point, my guidance counselor asked me if I had applied to any colleges. I told her no, I'd probably just go to Capital. I think that she knew that I had more in me than what I had shown on paper. She realized that I had the motivation to do better. At that point, she told me about the Dual College Enrollment Program at Eastern, and I was interested. "What do I have to do?" She told me the people at Eastern were coming to my high school to interview possible participants.

I almost missed the interview. It was close to the last week of high school, and I was in the hallway visiting with my teachers before I left for the day. One of my friends asked me "How did your interview go?"

"What interview?"

"For that program at Eastern."

I starting running down the hallway and was out of breath when I got to the interview room. Bob Fernandez, the representative from Quinebaug Valley Community College, asked me, "Are you Ismael?" I explained that I had forgotten about the interview, but he was still willing to talk to me. He gave me a lot of information on what college would be like, and he made me feel better about the finances. When he explained that I would start at a community college and go to Eastern part-time, I wondered if I would get to live on campus. Mr. Fernandez explained that I would live on campus, eat at the dining hall, attend events, and do everything that other Eastern students did.

Depending on how I did at Quinebaug and if the professors thought I was ready to step up, I would start full-time at Eastern in the spring. More important, there was funding available so that I didn't have to pay for anything in the first semester. Now it was simply a matter of whether or not they would take me.

BE PATIENT!

I was nervous and excited at the same time. What if I didn't get in? I hadn't applied to any other schools, so if I didn't get into the program, I would have to go to Capital. I waited for my acceptance letter from Eastern, and it didn't come. "Where's my letter? Didn't I get accepted?"

I called my guidance counselor and asked if she had heard anything from the people at Eastern. "Did they say I'm not accepted? Did I get a letter at school? What's going on?"

"You just have to be patient," she said. "I don't know what's going on, but just be patient."

A few days later I received my acceptance letter, and it said, "Congratulations." Once I saw that, I stopped reading and went to tell my mother. It brought tears to her eyes. It was such a happy moment. We ended up going out to dinner—me, my mother, and my brothers. It was such a good feeling to know that I'm going to be the first person in our family to graduate from college, because my sister passed away before she could graduate.

Knowing where I came from, from having so little to having a huge experience like this put in front of me was very humbling. I didn't want to abuse what I was being given. Since that first day when I received my letter of acceptance, I have tried to live up to what the program expected out of me.

BUILDING BONDS

I worked hard in my first semester at Quinebaug and transferred into Eastern as a full-time student that following January. I lived in Burr Hall my freshman year. It was great. We had one small common room where we all hung out. We had movie nights, a Super Bowl party, lots of fun things there. It was a place to get to know people. There was always someone playing the guitar or piano. People would be dancing. Plus, our doors were always open—you got to know everyone on your floor. In the bigger dorms, you don't know who the other kids are.

In my sophomore and junior years, I lived in the high-rise apartments on campus. It felt more like a home; we had a kitchen and I could cook for myself. I bonded immediately with my roommates on Facebook. We decorated our rooms together. We would watch basketball on TV with our friends, have X-Box tournaments, cook meals together. For my junior year, I kept the apartment but had a whole new set of roommates. It was totally new people all over again, but I was fine with having to meet new people. The way I see it, I may be able to help them, or they can help me.

LIKE A SECOND FAMILY

I was determined to make the most of the campus experience. I joined the Organization of Latin American Students (OLAS). It was good to have Hispanic students around whom I could relate to during my first months on campus. It was like being in my home neighborhood but with a different kind of support, because all the kids in OLAS are here to study and succeed.

I was OLAS treasurer as a junior, and I am still a member. When I first came in for summer orientation before my freshman year, Mike Pina was my student orientation counselor. I was pretty quiet, and he reached out to me. He encouraged me to join the club. We really don't consider ourselves a club; we are a family. We share a common culture, and we support one another as friends. Last week, we went to Rocky Neck Beach for a cookout. Now I reach out to the freshmen in OLAS. I help them come out of their shells, so they can get comfortable on campus. It's exciting as an upperclassman to see the freshmen getting used to being at Eastern. I am also in Habitat for Humanity this semester. I am not able to do as much, given my schedule, but I am trying to find time to help out as much as possible.

Even after four years, OLAS still feels like my second family. Professor Letterman, who is the OLAS advisor, sponsors dinners every Thursday night, which is a time for us to get together and socialize. Dr. Letterman is like having a second mom on campus. She makes you feel at home and is always trying to help. She likes to share research on careers and is always looking for ways for us to develop as individuals, students, and professionals. She is a psychology professor, so she talks all the time about society, about how it is changing, and about opportunities for us as Latinos. To be able to come here and have another sense of family has made college a lot easier for me. It made me more comfortable on campus, and I learned about other student clubs.

I also joined Men Achieving Leadership, Excellence, and Success (MALES). It does a lot of community service, and it reminded me of my Moylan Mastermind days in high school. In MALES, I have met some great friends. It is also where I have learned the importance of professional appearance and behavior. In MALES meetings, everyone acts like a mature adult and focuses on the business at hand. Now, when I go to a meeting or an interview, I know how to look professional and be mature.

MALES has helped me to become a leader on campus and be able to speak out more, as has OLAS. I have learned to voice my opinion instead of being timid about having to say something. Both OLAS and MALES have helped me mature as a college student. Even during my freshman year, I started to come out of my shell. When the residence hall elections came up, I decided to run for president of my hall. Mike Pina helped me improve my speech, and I ended up winning the election.

PHILOSOPHY AS ART

The course that I had the toughest time with as a freshman was philosophy. I never really understood it, no matter how much I paid attention. The professor challenged us to think. When we got into the topic of religion, he would ask, "What is God?" Someone would say, "God is the father of Jesus" or "God is a higher being." And the professor would ask, "How do you know he exists?" It was interesting to listen to but hard for me to absorb, and I would drift off. I started drawing pictures on the back of our assignment papers and turning those in.

The professor saw that I was struggling, so he pulled me aside, pointed to the set of my drawings on his desk, and asked, "Are these your emotions during class?" I said yes. I was drawing little silly faces, faces that were just empty. "You are going through these emotions right here in class?" He said that he saw my drawings as my interpretation of the discussions that were occurring in class. "You are creating a whole scene of what you are verbally hearing, and you're just reinterpreting it into art. If you can write down at least a paragraph of whatever we're talking about and then draw a picture on the back, I can grade you on it because it's work that you are doing." So he made philosophy a lot easier on me. It wasn't as difficult anymore, because I had another way to explain myself without having to use words.

WHERE THE PROFESSORS REMEMBER YOUR NAME

I really like the fact that so many of the professors at Eastern are hands-on. They will stay after the class to help you, even outside their office hours, or give you extra time to work on assignments. My web design professor, Kelly Carrington, was good about explaining the technical processes and would stop the class to help individual students. Other professors are like that also.

Amanda Lebel is great. She teaches printmaking. We had to buy tools for the class, and I had registered late. She said, "Use my tools"; she also gave me some printing paper. She told me, "Just pay me back when you can," which I did. We formed a bond, a trusting relationship. I enjoyed her class and was comfortable accepting her critiques to improve my work.

I took economics with Professor Clifford in my first semester. It opened up my eyes to the way that the world works—business, finance, industry. I just saw her last week, and it seems like yesterday when I had her, but it was four years ago. It was great to catch up with a former professor who still remembers who I am. At a big university, they don't remember you, or perhaps they never even knew you. At Eastern, our classes are, at most twenty to twenty-five, so the professors get to know you.

I also took an independent study class with Spanish professor Augustin Bernal. We focused on Cuba and Puerto Rico—the music, food, culture, economies, and politics of the islands. The last week of class, we talked about the statehood issue in Puerto Rico; it's very controversial. We had an intense discussion, and Professor Bernal respected our differing opinions on the topic. I always looked forward to going to his class; he has a great sense of humor and keeps things positive.

One thing that I have learned in all my classes is that when a project is complicated and consists of a lot of elements, it consumes time. I also have a job and club responsibilities. I have learned how to prioritize. Sometimes, you just have to cut out the social activities and focus on getting the work done.

SUPPORT OUTSIDE THE CLASSROOM

The professors at Eastern are very supportive, even if you aren't taking a class with them. Dr. Letterman encourages me to bring my papers to her for advice and input. If we just need to talk, her office is always open. Every semester, she gives me her card with her office hours on it—like I don't already have six of them! She even gets us big calendars with every month on it to put down important dates, like finals week, meetings, and such.

Indira Petoskey, who initially ran the dual enrollment program, has also been wonderful. When I first met her, it was funny, because my brother used to date her foster daughter. We recognized each other when I first met her. I said, "You've been to my house before!" It was just weird. Dr. Petoskey is always there to help me, whether it's lending me $5 to buy art store supplies or giving me a ride home. She calls me "Hijo," which is "son" in Spanish.

Dr. Walter Diaz has also been right there for me. He is the dean of students and another OLAS advisor. When I arrived on campus, he would kid me about cutting my braids. I never took him seriously until I went to a conference in New Jersey. I was dressed up, but when I looked in the mirror, I realized that I wasn't professional looking, so I cut the braids off. There have been times these past four years that I wanted to quit. Dr. Diaz would encourage me, but he would also say, "It's your decision." He has always given me good advice, but he always respects me and my decisions.

BALANCING TWO WORLDS

I stayed on campus most weekends during my first year and went home only for Christmas break and Thanksgiving. Then I didn't go home again until spring break. I missed my family, and I know that they felt the same way. When I did go home, some of my friends in the neighborhood were mad at me for not being around as much. They would want to go out and party, but I just wanted to hang out at home. These were the friends who had been leading me down the wrong path.

My other friends were proud of me. They realized that I hadn't changed in terms of our relationship. "You're the only one of the group who's doing something good; you're in college while I'm struggling to find a decent-paying job out there." Some of my friends will come to campus to see me. About five of them just came to campus for the Wale concert. They see what I have here, and it feels good that they were willing to visit me here. We will go out to eat, play basketball, watch a movie, or go to a party. These are the people that I trust; they haven't changed, and they know that I haven't changed.

I know that some of my friends have been influenced by what I have been able to accomplish at Eastern. My friend Flacc is going to Capital Community College. He tells me that he's planning on transferring to a university after two years. It's cool to know your friends want to be like you, going to college and starting a career.

Both my brothers have always been supportive of me, and both say that they want to go to college also. One of my brothers struggles with school, but I keep telling him to go to Capital Community College. My little sister is already at Capital. She has two kids, so it isn't easy, but she takes night classes and is trying to get her nursing assistant certification. I hope that she ends up getting her four-year degree, too.

JOINING THE GROWN-UPS

For the two dual enrollment classes entering in 2011 and 2012, I was asked to go with the Eastern and Quinebaug Valley Community College staff back to Hartford Public High School to be part of the interviewing team. It was like being one of the grown-ups! I think that the idea was to have someone talking to the high school students whom they could relate to. When I go back to Hartford High now and talk to the students there, I share my experiences and tell them how it was for me when I was in high school.

During the interviews, I look for students whom I can look in the eye and know that they can succeed in the program, just by the way that they talk. We also look at their grades. I look for someone who is motivated, someone who really wants to go to college and make something of themselves. The most recent cohort told us that it was even willing to take summer and winter break courses if it had to. That was a big plus on those students' part.

I was in the first group of dual enrollment students from Hartford Public High School. The program was new, so they were still trying to figure out what worked best. Every year, the people who run the program sit down with the students at the end of the year to talk with them about how to make this program better. It's a great program. Eastern has been willing to improve it, and all of the changes are for the better. I don't know of any other schools doing this.

WHAT IF?

Ever since I moved to Hartford, I have always lived near Park Street. It's the main drag on the south end of Hartford. There are always things happening—fights, drugs, gunshots all the time, glass breaking, people arguing. If I hadn't come to Eastern, my life would have been a lot different. Going to school at Eastern has allowed me to get away from all the street-related problems that I had back home. Selling drugs, getting into fights, getting arrested—that was the future I was looking at in Hartford. Over the past few years, I have lost four or five friends from street fighting—getting stabbed or shot, getting locked up for selling drugs. Some of them were my close friends, and I realize that it could have been me.

I remember seeing the struggles that my mother and father faced when I was younger to put food on the table and pay the bills. When I have my own family, I don't want anyone to have to go through the same things that I went through: not being able to take a hot shower, not being able to watch TV; not being able to turn on the light when you're scared at night—I know what the word "struggle" means. I see my niece and nephew, and I don't want them growing up like that.

CAREER PLANS

Hopefully, I'll graduate next year. With a degree in graphic design, I hope to have a variety of options. I think that I want to focus on advertising. There is so much opportunity in that field. I enjoy creating logos. I also like to design T-shirts. I work in the Intercultural Center, and I am trying to use my design skills to help promote our events. We have five big events coming up, and T-shirts are always a good draw to get people to come to an event.

There are other areas of graphic design that I am interested in—game design, web sites; there are a lot of possibilities. Someday, I would like to save up enough money to open up my own clothing business and sneaker store. It's just something that I have always wanted to do. My sister-in-law is an accountant, so she can handle the finances.

LEARNING TO BE ME

I have learned to be a leader on campus, to voice my opinion more in the organizations that I am involved in. I have seen myself maturing as a college student at Eastern, and now I can be a role model on campus that others can look up to. I can be somebody that somebody else would remember on campus.

I have learned that I'm more than just where I come from. I'm more than just the streets that I grew up on. I'm more than just the friends that I hung around with. I'm more than who I was growing up. Because of Dr. Núñez, students from my neighborhood and I are being given a four-year university education and the complete college life experience. I cannot thank her enough for being willing to help us.

EIGHT

Whitley Mingo, Class of 2013

Every little small gesture that was made for me in the program really changed my life!

GETTING A FOOTHOLD

My parents were both born in Guyana, and each had a tough life growing up there. My mother got as far as tenth grade and took typing and shorthand in secretarial school. My father also went as far as tenth grade and learned to become a mechanic. My mom was the oldest sibling in her family, so she had to work; all her other siblings were allowed to attend high school. She learned how to make pastries and create her own business.

When she was twenty, my mom's family sent her to Canada to help her aunt take care of her child. But she was undocumented and sent back to Guyana. She returned to Canada while her papers were being processed so that she could live in the United States legally. After coming to New York as a legal resident, she returned to Guyana to marry my dad. They then immigrated to Connecticut.

My mother became a live-in maid and would send money back to Guyana to help care for her family. My father had a trade education as a skilled mechanic. He became what we call a "fix-it guy" in my neighborhood; today he works as a mechanic at a Lexus car dealership.

FINDING INSPIRATION AT HOME

My parents divorced when I was three. Even though my sister, my two brothers, and I grew up with my mom, my dad has always lived nearby. I got to see my dad frequently, but he wasn't living with us. We always had a relationship with him though.

So my mom was single, working hard to support us—sometimes at more than one job and often at night—and she always found ways to make sure that we were able to do what other kids did. I was able to take dancing lessons, and she made sure that we were involved in other activities, like taking field trips with the rest of the kids in school. Even though we didn't have much money, she found ways to see that we got what we needed to achieve. I think I get my drive from my mom, and she has helped me to always have faith that I will find a way to reach my goals.

My mom didn't go to college, but she took adult education classes at Hartford Public High School at the same time that my sister was going to Weaver High School; they graduated the same year. My mom was about thirty-six when she got her human services diploma! Then she took nursing courses at places like the Capital Region Education Council and got her certification as a nursing assistant. I am so proud of her for that. Her commitment to improving herself is why I wanted to go to college—to achieve a little bit more because of how hard she has worked to get to where she is today.

She didn't want my sister to graduate from high school with a mom who did not have a high school diploma herself. In addition, my sister would come home and need help with her homework. My mom was always good at math, and when she saw Stephanie's homework, she saw that she could do it. She realized that she needed to go back to school and get it done. She had the opportunity that she had not had when she was a teenager in Guyana, so she was determined to make the most of it. This is a lesson that has stuck with me ever since.

FOLLOWING IN MY SISTER'S FOOTSTEPS

I am the youngest of four. My sister is the oldest, and she was the first to go to college. She went to Providence College on a full scholarship based on her academic record at Weaver High School. She has a master's degree in health policy and management and a master's degree in human resource management. She works in the health department at Georgia State University. She wants to get her registered nursing degree and start her own practice as a nurse practitioner.

She is the reason that I wanted to come to Eastern. Everything I have done is because of my sister. I did everything the way that she did it when I was growing up. She is thirteen years older than me; I was born when she was starting high school. It's almost like having another mom. When I was growing up, we didn't really have a sister-like bond; I always saw her as an adult figure because she's so much older than me.

After college, she was hired by AMICA Insurance, which gave her a place to live and a car, and she moved to New Jersey. When she came home, she would encourage me—"How are you coming with your homework?" or "Why don't you read this book?"

She saw the way that things happened in other families in our neighborhood, and she would help guide me so that I would stay on the right path.

I WAS DANCING AND THEN . . .

We moved to East Hartford when I started third grade; it had better schools than my old neighborhood in Hartford. I went to school there until my sophomore year, when I was accepted into the Academy of the Arts for Ballet. I transferred back to Hartford Public High School because I could attend the Academy for the Arts for free there; if I stayed at East Hartford High School, it would have cost us $3,000 a year for me to take ballet, and we didn't have that much money. So I transferred to Hartford High. My brother lived across the street, so it was perfect. I attended regular classes for half the day, and I then I would go to the academy to dance the remainder of the day. I loved to dance, but I wasn't at the point where I was committed in my mind to pursue dancing as a career; it was more like a hobby. The idea was out there, but I was just enjoying the experience at the time. When I was a senior in high school, I fell and hurt my knee. I realized that I wasn't going to be able to support myself as a professional dancer, and I began thinking that I should look into nursing.

A NEW START AT HARTFORD HIGH

When I first got to Hartford High School, I was frightened. The high school is in a tough part of town, and I didn't know anyone. Plus, I was put into AP classes and honors math, and I was getting F's. I shouldn't have been in those classes, and finally I was moved to classes that I could handle.

As soon as I was put in classes that I could manage, I felt better. I also liked the teachers at Hartford High—they truly take an interest in their students. They see what you're good at and encourage you and talk to you and help you with whatever issues you might have. They keep you motivated so that you can attend college, and they encourage you: "You can do it . . . you need to go to college."

One teacher in particular—Mrs. Hucklee—took me under her wing and told me that she thought that I could succeed in college. She would check in with me to see how I was doing in other classes. I also would eat lunch with her. I would go to Mrs. Hucklee's room every day, and she would tell me that I needed to make friends. I would tell her that I was fine eating with her, but she would insist that I make friends. So I met one girl who became my friend, and I would go to my brother's house across the street for lunch. I would find my way out of school and go eat at his house and then find my way back into school.

One thing that helped me in high school, I think, was the fact that I had a lot of different experiences and influences. I danced at the Academy for the Arts; my church is very diverse, as opposed to being heavily ethnic; and my siblings and I got to go to summer camps and other activities—some of them sponsored by our church—so I didn't end up hanging out with the girls who got into trouble. I was one of the "nice girls"; I liked to meet new people and make new friends.

FOLLOWING MY SISTER'S LEAD

With my sister having such success in college, I always assumed that I would find a way to get to college, even though I had no idea how I was going to pay for it. Finding the money to stay in college was the biggest puzzle piece that was needed to make my life the way that I wanted it to be. I didn't know how it was going to happen, but I knew that I was going. I think that came from being around friends who also wanted to go to college; I just felt it my right—I had to go to college. Everyone was applying to school, but no one spent much time talking about financial issues and how to afford college.

In my senior year in high school, my mom moved to Atlanta to help my sister Stephanie with her children. She was married, and her husband and she both worked, so my mother moved down there to help them out. During my senior year, I lived with my aunt and sometimes with my brother and his girlfriend. I figured that I would apply to colleges in Georgia and move there to be with my mom and my sister. So I applied to Georgia State and to Emory, which was one of the schools that the faculty at Hartford High had mentioned to me. My math SAT score was low, so I had to retake the math part. I needed to do well, but I was still having trouble with math, and my scores still were not that good. I was given conditional acceptance at Georgia State but would have to pay out-of-state tuition, and my family simply couldn't afford it.

I DISCOVER EASTERN

At that point, my guidance counselor introduced me to the Dual College Enrollment Program at Eastern. We were sitting across the table from each other, and she said, "Let's look at this program at Eastern. I don't think you should put all your hopes on planning to attend college in Georgia, because being an out-of-state student is very expensive."

At first, I didn't want to go to Eastern. I had never heard of the school until the day that she gave me the informational packet about the Dual College Enrollment Program. I didn't even know where Willimantic was. I had not heard of Western Connecticut State University either; I only knew about Central. I told my guidance counselor that I didn't know where Eastern was, and she started laughing. I was scared, but she said that the faculty and staff at Eastern were very friendly and that I should give it a shot.

So I went to the interview, and I told the people from Eastern all about my life, my school experiences, my interests—everything—and I decided right then that I was going to prove myself. It was a good thing that I was chosen because I wouldn't have been able to go to Georgia State, and I would have ended up not being able to go to college at all.

The Dual College Enrollment Program at Eastern was a great opportunity for me because it has worked very hard to help students like me pay for education. Without that help, my mom and I were never going to have the money to pay for my college education. At Eastern, the faculty and staff are there to help students graduate in four years. A lot of the people that I went to school with who I thought were smarter than me didn't finish college, are still in school, or have dropped out and joined the military or taken whatever job they could find.

BURR WAS A BLAST!

I was a member of the first Dual College Enrollment Program cohort, and we had a special bond. We studied together; we hung out together; we really stuck together. We all lived in Burr Hall—three floors: boys, girls, boys. It is an older dormitory, and we didn't have TVs in our rooms, so we were forced to go down to the common room to watch TV and engage with everyone else. There were nine of us, but none of the other students on campus knew that we were even in the Dual College Enrollment Program. We never talked about it to anyone else until our sophomore year, when the next cohort came in and talked about being in the program. Other students would ask, "How come you're not in any of our freshman classes?" I would just say we were taking different classes. So we did a good job of fitting in, which is what the people running the program wanted for us anyway.

It was different from city life in Hartford. It was a brand-new experience for all of us. We met students from many different places who had totally different lives from what we had experienced. In some of the larger dorms, students stick to their rooms, but in Burnap, we all got to know one another. I had a great freshman year. Plus, I knew another member of the cohort from my time at Hartford High, and I even had a fellow student who had attended East Hartford Middle School with me.

I cannot say enough about the experience of living on a college campus. I know people whom I went to school with who go to Capital Community College. They don't get the kind of experience that we got from living on campus. Living on campus forced me to be independent.

The people at Eastern really make the point that you are in charge of your own life. I had to learn about the entire college experience; my mom doesn't know anything about college. Financial aid, grades, what courses to take—I had to learn it all on my own. Of course, my sister had gone through the same experience, but she was busy with her life in Atlanta, so it was up to me.

A NEW WORLD THIRTY MILES AWAY

Initially, living on Eastern's campus was scary for me, coming from Hartford and East Hartford. I know that sounds funny—actually, I was joking about this with friends at dinner one time. Sometimes we had to walk to class in the dark, or it was dark when we got out of class. We were more comfortable walking around Hartford at night and feeling safe. Eventually, we understood that the Eastern campus is lit up at night; the university police are always around for security; and we are taught to walk in groups, not alone. So you begin to realize that you don't have to be frightened.

Another thing that you have to get used to in coming to campus from the inner city is the diversity. In Hartford, most of the kids at my school were Hispanic—Puerto Ricans mostly—and African American. It's a bit of a culture shock to live on a campus with kids from all over—Caucasians, kids from other states and other countries, as well as Caribbean students of African descent, and Hispanics from many other countries. At the end of my time on campus, this diversity of people helped me grow up and be more independent, but at first, I missed my mom a lot. She would come and visit sometimes, and I'd call her and talk to her, but I still missed her. It was hard, and it wasn't easy to find a way to get back home to see her, even though it's only thirty miles away. Once I was able to get a car, it was easier to visit home, and at the same time, I was becoming more involved with student life at Eastern and more comfortable living on campus.

WRITING HAS ALWAYS BEEN MY CHALLENGE

I was in the college prep track at East Hartford High School. My standardized test scores were always good, but my grades were only average. My writing has always been a challenge. If we were taking an essay test in class, I would always be the last one to finish the test, and my essays were always late. While I was in East Hartford, I didn't receive a lot of help. And of course, as anyone in the field of education knows, the ability to write well is a function of one's ability to read and comprehend. My problem has always been that I don't always fully understand the topic or issue being discussed. This has been true ever since I was in grade school in East Hartford. In fact, I was held back in the third grade because of this. I never felt that the teachers there were willing or able to help me. Most of the kids "got it," and I always felt that I was a burden in class. It became a matter of high anxiety for me, and I ended up just sitting there quietly rather than asking for extra help. I would turn to other students — rather than the teachers — to figure out the answers.

At Hartford Public High School, I was given extra time; we had tutors to help; and the Career Center and Guidance Office did a great job of preparing us for college. But my writing skills still weren't where they needed to be when I started at Eastern. I never really felt like someone was truly interested in helping me improve my writing until my anthropology professor at Eastern said, "You seem to need extra time on your papers."

LEARNING LEADERSHIP SKILLS ON CAMPUS

One of my favorite activities at Eastern was being vice president of the campus chapter of the National Organization for Women. We did a lot to empower women on our campus. I helped set up a trip to see Anita Baker sing in New York City. We worked to provide opportunities for women on campus to improve their self-esteem, such as hosting body image workshops. It really made me appreciate being a woman and having a leadership role on campus. The National Organization for Women was all about women empowering one another, giving themselves strength to deal with the real world. It gave me the confidence that I can be successful and have a professional career.

I was also involved with the African Club. We coordinated field trips and organized fashion shows on campus. We all come from a neighborhood somewhere, and sometimes we play it safe and stay within our own social circle and familiar territory. The African Club forced me to reach out and make connections with students from Zambia, Europe, and other countries, as well as from all over the United States. I still stay in contact with them.

IT'S A BIG WORLD OUT THERE

While at Eastern, I was also fortunate to study abroad on two occasions. My friend Nana is from Zambia. One summer, we went together to London and Paris with two communication professors and other students. We met one of Nana's childhood pals in London. It was great; I didn't feel like a tourist! We visited the London Jazz Café and lots of different restaurants. Our communication class also visited advertising agencies like McCann-Erickson, as well as museums on advertising and architecture. We visited Big Ben, art markets, and Trafalgar Square. The English are cultured yet diverse. The lifestyle there is very different—I encountered new music, fashion, food—a whole new world. It really opened up my viewpoint and my horizons.

We also visited Paris, and I went to the Louvre on my own. My brother, who is a big *Da Vinci Code* fan, was jealous! I also visited Notre Dame, walked on several of the bridges that cross the Seine River, climbed the Eiffel Tower, and toured the palace and gardens of Versailles—it was all amazing.

In France, they expect you to speak French. In England, it was easier. The monetary conversion was easier to work with, and I also learned a lot about advertising. Guyana was owned by the British, so I was able to connect some of my family's personal history to my time in England.

I also had an opportunity to go to Jamaica during spring break my junior year with Professor David Stoloff. We spent a week working in the schools there, and I was able to observe how life at home affects the learning that takes place in school. It is clear to me that if we want to help kids living in poverty to succeed in school, we have to help the entire family.

I LEARNED TO SPEAK UP

One thing that I am glad that I learned at Eastern is to literally speak up for myself and be able to approach things calmly. I learned not to make snap judgments but rather spend some time thinking about the issue so that I can take an educated position. We all represent ourselves by what we say, and I am proud that I can hold my own ground in a conversation. I'm really proud of myself for finding my motivation here at Eastern. I discovered that I can do whatever I decide I want to do. It's not really about having money; it's about being determined to do something. I have friends from Hartford, from New Haven, from other tough neighborhoods who didn't have the best upbringing, but they're president of the Student Government Association now. All things are possible. At Eastern, my friends in the dual enrollment program and I have discovered that we can really change, and we've watched one another grow, from the first day we were on campus to the day we graduated.

SUPPORT FROM ALL SIDES

I am not saying that my college experience was easy. If you had asked someone, "How many times did Whitley come to your office and say she was going to drop out?" they would tell you it was at least ten. I was always complaining, something was hard, I was ready to give up, I wanted to cry—but no one would let me give up.

I received a lot of support through the Academic Services Center at Eastern. For instance, I had a peer tutor from Norway—Kim Thomassen-Strand—who would help me with my writing. I would meet with her, and she taught me to create an outline of what I wanted to say. We would review the outline, and then I would leave and fill it in. I would come back and show Kim what I had done, and then I would actually write the paper. I would bring it back to my tutor, and she would help me edit it.

I also received one-on-one math support from my math teacher at Quinnebaug Valley Community College during my first semester in the DCEP program. I never liked math until that year, but I actually got an A in math—who would have thought? I ended up practicing math back in my bedroom—who does that? My math professor at Quinnebaug was good. She was trained to work with adult students, because adults think differently than young children. Her way of explaining mathematical concepts really helped me to see how math works—literally for the first time in my life.

Another unexpected source of support was my freshman roommate. She was an English major and was studying to be a teacher. My English teacher at Quinnebaug also was very helpful. She was strict about using the right punctuation, and she taught me the proper way of making citations on my papers; it was something that not everyone paid attention to, but she made a big deal about getting it right.

Of course, the financial support that I have received from the Eastern Connecticut State University Foundation and the university to help me pay for college has made all the difference—without that support, I wouldn't have been able to come to Eastern at all.

I WANTED TO HELP PEOPLE . . . BUT HOW?

One of the important decisions that you have to make when you go to college is to decide on your major. At first, I wanted to be a nurse. I was clearly influenced by my mom and my sister, who have always been my two major role models. My mother is a certified nursing assistant, and even though my sister has two master's degrees, she's going back to school for nursing. But when I got to Eastern, I was told that it didn't have a nursing program. I started to talk with my professors, and I realized that I like working with people who have issues. It turns out that I'm really good at helping people, so I wanted to go into social work. However, at Eastern you need to be accepted into the social work program and take certain classes prior to getting in. I would have had to take additional classes and be at Eastern another year if I wanted to get into the program. My scholarships wouldn't cover for me another year, so I decided to major in sociology instead. I can get my graduate degree in social work later if I want to. I think that I want to be a social worker in a hospital or somewhere else in the medical field. I have a friend whose mom is a social worker for pediatric oncology patients at the Cleveland Clinic; she has a perfect personality for it, but it must be the hardest job in the world.

I was very fortunate to have some outstanding professors in the sociology department. Professor Dennis Canterbury expects a lot from his students, but he was always willing to help me and other students. His classes were insightful, and while I enjoyed my time in class, years later I am still discovering how much he taught me. I learned about globalization, social theory, and much more. He is also from Guyana, and that helped me also.

Professor Cara Bergstrom-Lynch was another of my favorite teachers. Her classes are not structured to focus on just one thing. She would talk about broader topics—the sociology of families, how gender influences a person's life. We would talk about the social conditions that make it difficult for the African American population to be successful. I was able to see what has to happen in my own life to change outcomes.

GROWING INTO YOURSELF

Another benefit of going to school at Eastern was the fact you could practice your major off campus—in my case, through an internship. I worked in a program called "Nurturing Families" in Willimantic. I helped get donations for the program. I would have phone conversations with young mothers—mostly single first-time moms. They didn't have a lot of support systems. The program focused on family life and education, and it helped reaffirm my interest in working with infants and mothers, as well as first-time or pregnant mothers. If we can provide these young women with the knowledge and tools that they need to survive, then we can help ensure that their babies won't be taken away from them.

I also stayed on campus during the summer and worked in the Child and Family Development Resource Center. It was a great place to be if you want to work with kids—a perfect setting.

MY BROTHERS ARE MAKING THEIR OWN WAY

My older brother didn't go on to college—school wasn't for him. In fact, at one point, he was expelled from high school for 180 days—a full year! It was one of those things where another kid wrote some graffiti on a locker, and my brother took the blame for it. The police actually came to school and arrested him for something that he didn't do. But my mom made him finish high school after the suspension was lifted.

For a while, he got caught up in the Hartford young male lifestyle. One night, he and a friend were outside a bar in Hartford, and his friend was being attacked. My brother tried to help, and he ended up getting shot. He recovered, but I think he realized that the life he was leading was jeopardizing not only his life but his loved ones as well.

He figured it out, and today he has a family—a wife and two young sons. He is an ironworker in Hartford and has worked on a number of major construction projects: he worked on the Connecticut Science Center, St. Francis Hospital's Emergency Room wing, and the Child Development Center at Goodwin College.

His two sons are six and seven years old now. They came to my graduation, and I let them try on my cap and gown. I told them, "You are going to go to college too when you grow up." That's what I want for them. I tell them to do well in school, to study hard. They see me and my sister, and I think that they know that school is a good thing, not a bad thing.

My other brother wasn't sure what he wanted to do for a long time. He worked at East Hartford High School for a while, but he was just floating. Now he is going to Eastern, just like I did. He initially went to a trade school, and after seeing how well I was doing at Eastern, he decided to give college a chance. Even though he's twenty-six, he knows that it doesn't matter when you attend school as long as you do it. He is majoring in math—he takes after my mom!—and he loves to read. He is always reading—he'll stay in the car reading while the rest of us are in the grocery store. He will open a book no matter where he is! I think my going to college motivated him to see if he could also do it; it made me feel good knowing that I could inspire him the way that my sister inspired me.

TODAY AND TOMORROW

I would like to become a social worker in a hospital or somewhere else in a medical-related field. I also have come to realize that many people working in our cities can't relate to the African American lifestyle or family orientation and the upbringing of the people they are trying to help. They end up judging their patients and clients based on their own experiences. Perhaps they have raised their own children in normal sur-roundings, and they have no idea what it is like to have your child taken away from you or to visit your child in an institutional setting. I think that I can help in those situations; if social service agency clients have someone who can relate to their lives, to their neighborhoods, to their upbringing, it will be easier for them. I can see myself going to the home of some young African American mother who is high risk, knocking on the door, and having her open the door to see someone who is also of African heritage. I think that it will be more comfortable for her to be able to talk to me, knowing that she won't be judged. She might be more comfortable to open up to me. So that will be my personal way to give back and make a difference. I would like to start in the Hartford area first because that's where I'm from and I can refine my skills. At some point, I think that I would like to move to the Washington, DC, area and become the coordinator of a program that helps young mothers and their infants.

Right now, I am working in Hartford in a Maternal and Infants Out-reach program. I have nine clients right now and will eventually have up to fifteen. The program is located throughout the city of Hartford. We network with churches, schools, nonprofits, and social agencies. I love it. I have always wanted to work with mothers and infants. This is great practice before I become a social worker in a hospital. My vision is to apply for the master's program in social work at the University of Con-necticut next year.

LOOKING BACK

I have so many fond memories of my time at Eastern. In a very real way, Eastern helped me find out who I am. So many of the professors went out of their way to help me. They saw something in me and made me feel that I could do this. I realized that I could graduate like everyone else; I was capable of doing the work. The volunteer opportunities that I partici-pated in, the people who touched me from my freshman year to gradua-tion, including my roommates in the dorms—I learned so much from the people around me. Living and studying on campus also helped me ma-ture as an adult—how to find a job, how to manage my life. And all the opportunities that I had to learn outside the classroom—through intern-ships and study abroad—really helped prepare me for my future.

Some of the people involved with the Dual College Enrollment Pro-gram might not realize the importance of what they are doing for stu-dents in the program. But every little small gesture that was made for the program really changed my life. It may not have seemed like that big of a deal, but it really was. This program has improved the lives of every student who has been a part of it. It is a big step in helping and showing what is out there and what individuals are capable of.

* * *

Whitley is applying for graduate school at the University of Connecticut for fall 2014.

NINE
Todd Aviles

Todd made up his mind that he wanted a different life for himself, and Eastern has helped him do that.
—Charlene Senteio, guidance counselor, Hartford Public High School

STARTING OFF ON THE WRONG FOOT

My mother was born in Puerto Rico and grew up in the Bronx. My dad was born and raised in Brooklyn. Eventually, my parents moved to Hartford, where I was born.

I am the oldest of three children. During my elementary school years, I was always considered a leader by my teachers. I did well academically and fit in well with my classmates. Then my parents got divorced when I was in sixth grade, and it took a big toll on me. Even though I was mature for my age and knew a lot of things that many sixth graders don't know, going through a divorce is a pretty big deal for any kid. I was the oldest in our family, and that made it even more difficult. I love both my parents, so to see them fall apart and find myself choosing sides tore me up. I would have animosity toward my mother to the point of having arguments and rebelling against her and her new boyfriend. It was on multiple occasions, even continuing into high school. It was a difficult time.

When I got to high school, there were still issues with the divorce, and I started smoking marijuana. I did it throughout high school, until my senior year. It took me away from who I used to be and what I used to stand for. In my sophomore year, I failed five classes straight—all year long. I really didn't care.

I got kicked out of my first high school—the University of Hartford High School of Science and Engineering. Then I went to Hartford Public

High School and got kicked out of summer school twice—on the first day and the second.

At some point, I decided that I really didn't want to continue the path I was on. Over that junior summer when I got kicked out of summer school, I started asking myself, "Why am I doing this?" I realized that I was running away from my problems, but you can only run away so far. So I told myself that I needed to stop running. In my senior year, I almost had a panic attack, and I stopped smoking pot.

During my junior year, I had been arrested for breach of peace. One afternoon, everyone was outside of school at the end of the day—yelling, being loud, the usual. Like everyone else, I was being obnoxious, so a policeman stopped me and said, "Put your hands behind your back." I resisted arrest, and the policeman slammed me on the ground. After that, one of my teachers, Mr. Ramos, introduced me to Frankie Agosto, who was a Peace Builder. That's how I got involved in Peace Builders and things started turning around.

GETTING BACK ON TRACK

Peace Builders is a community service-based program run by the Compass Youth Collaborative that works with at-risk youths in Hartford. Peace Builders are former gang members themselves, trying to do right. I got a job as a Junior Peace Builder, working with older Peace Builders who work on the streets to reduce gang violence within the neighborhoods. The Junior Peace Builders do community service, go through life skills development, and take field trips to get exposed to new experiences.

I got a stipend as a Junior Peace Builder and was working hard, feeling engaged in my community. It meant a lot to have a job. From there, I started working as an after-school professional youth developer at Naylor Middle School. It is also a Compass Youth Collaborative program. Two projects that I created that I especially enjoyed working on with the kids was "i-Hero," where they had to create a hero figure and then produce a comic book based on that hero, and "Space 101," when we learned about space and star systems. When you talk about the vastness of space, you begin to appreciate how special and unique life on Earth is.

One other thing that really helped me turn things around in high school was the social worker I began seeing in my junior year of high school. Her name was Amanda. I'll never forget her—she has a very special place in my heart. She helped me out so much. I would go to see her every day. I was referred to her because one day in Spanish class, I lost my cool. We were doing an art project, and there weren't enough scissors to go around. I like to take my time on my artwork, but everyone was rushing me—I lost my head and bolted from class. Who did I run into but the dean of students. He told me that he wanted me to talk with someone. I said no, but he kept coming back to me with the same thing: "I want you to talk with someone." I gave in, and that's how I met Amanda. We started to meet, and I opened up to her. I began to realize that I was my own worst enemy. I started to work on myself, being part of Junior Peace Builders, turning my life around.

In my senior year in high school, I had an opportunity that first gave me the sense that I might have talent as a public speaker. We had a debate on gun control, and it was broadcast by one of the local television stations. I felt that my argument and presentation were strong, and the feedback I got from people was very positive. One of my teachers, Mr. Nieves, pulled me to the side and said, "You have great potential. Let me help you become even better at public speaking." What has happened at Eastern since then has just reaffirmed that I have a gift that I need to find a way to share with the world.

OPPORTUNITY KNOCKS

During high school, my goal was pretty simple—finish and graduate. I was thinking that maybe I would go into the military, but I knew that, at the end of the day, no matter what path I chose, I was determined to graduate from high school. No one on my mother's side of the family had finished high school, so I am the first one to finish high school and the first to go to college.

Going to college was something that I thought about in my senior year, but I wasn't sure if I was ready. Originally, my friend Matt and I were going to sign up for the army together. Then one day, he said, "I don't know, I think I want to go to college." So of course, I said that I wanted to go to college too, even though I had no plan on how to do it. Funny enough, Matt still ended up going into the army.

I was naïve. I always wanted to go to New York, so I thought that maybe I should apply to New York University. But I procrastinated and didn't apply until it was too late. By March of my senior year, I was panicking. I applied to the University of Connecticut, but there was something about my SATs that was missing and I wasn't admitted.

It was about that time that my guidance counselor told me about the Dual College Enrollment Program at Eastern. It was like a life raft in the middle of the ocean. I was excited; I immediately filled in the application and wrote up my résumé. All the work that I had been doing throughout my senior year gave me confidence that I was a good candidate for the program.

The people from Eastern came to Hartford Public High School to interview us. I talked about all the work that I was doing in the community and how I was working with the kids at Naylor Middle School. And

I made sure that I made it clear that I really wanted to go to college somehow. Within a few days, my guidance counselor told me, "I got word back. You've been accepted into the program."

I was happy and overwhelmed. What is interesting is that I had visited Eastern during eighth grade and really didn't like it. I thought it wasn't cool. When I actually came to Eastern as a freshman in 2010, I realized that it was the right thing for me. I felt blessed to have this opportunity to go to college. I hadn't wanted to commute to community college; I wanted to go to a university. I knew that I could do it.

THE BURNAP CREW

When I got accepted into the Dual College Enrollment Program, I was so psyched that I packed my bags a month early. When I arrived on campus for the summer orientation program, I got lucky. My student orientation counselor was Eli Gomez, and he was so supportive. He also made me want to be a student orientation counselor, which I actually did after my freshman year.

During my freshman year, I lived in Burnap Hall, one of the older dormitories on campus, and I was lucky to be there. The older residence halls aren't set up as suites or apartments, so you are forced to go to the common lounge to meet other students. It was the number-one spot where we chilled. We would all be in there telling jokes, laughing at one another, doing homework, watching football games on TV. You got to know everyone in the building. I still love Burnap to this day. I got to know everyone, and we called our little group "the Burnap Crew." It was me, Johnny, Mohammad, Andrew, Vince, Jerry, and a few other people. We would go out bowling or get a bite to eat, and we tried to meet as many people as possible.

Then the summer came, and I was hired as a student orientation counselor. I got to help the new incoming freshmen get used to campus, comfortable with the system, familiar with the faces they were going to see in the fall, just like Eli Gomez did for me. I loved the entire experience. Everything that I did as an orientation counselor has prepared me for the work that I am doing now. It was the kind of work that could be applied to anything—people skills, communication skills, organizational skills, patience, being sure that you demonstrate your energy, motivation, and resilience.

BOOKS FIRST

The big thing that I have learned is that if I work hard, I can do this. They say that all you have to do is put your mind to it and you can do anything, and I think that it's true. I am keeping my grades up, which I am very proud of, and at the same time, I am very involved with activities on campus. I think that's a nice balance to have. I also enjoy the fact that each professor is different from the next. Sometimes you will have a professor who assigns a lot of work, and other professors will be more focused on team projects or what goes on in class.

I can think of a number of professors who have pushed me intellectually. I have really enjoyed Dennis Canterbury's sociology classes. He starts each class with a story; it's his way of getting the students comfortable in the room before we get to work. And he loves asking us, "What do you think?" In his classes, I get a chance to express myself. Debate and discussion are the best way that I learn, and I love how Dr. Canterbury approaches them. He creates a great atmosphere with his attitude—he's excited and prepared at the same time. We learn sociological theories like Durkheim's division of labor, the history of the discipline. Sociology is the scientific study of human interaction, either group behavior or how the individual relates to the group. We talk about what defines a group— similar interests, passions, behavior. If you want to be a leader, you need to understand interpersonal and group dynamics.

Basic Speech with Professor Curtis was a breakthrough course for me. My speech on how the Giants won the Super Bowl was one of my greatest moments. I am also interested in the possibility of life beyond our own planet. In Professor Luxemburg's College Writing class, I got to do an essay on extraterrestrial life. I was able to put a lot of information into five pages. My research reinforced my beliefs; I've been interested in the paranormal since high school.

IT'S A JUGGLING ACT

One of my challenges that I am working on is time management. I'm getting better at it. Some weeks everything is done on time—good to go—and some weeks, there's so much work that it's a juggling act. I have homework; I have my job; I have my club responsibilities; and I have my community service work. Time management is definitely my biggest challenge. I also struggle with my sleep cycle; like most college students, I could get more sleep.

I think for all the students at Eastern, the services that we have on hand to help us stay focused on our academics are like a giant safety net. I think that I have utilized every support service that we have here— career services, advising, financial aid, tutoring, and other support in the Academic Services Center. And there are so many people who take you under their wings and serve as formal or informal mentors—faculty, administrators, advisors, career counselors. I just know that if I need help, I can turn to a number of different people, and they will be there for me.

LIFE ON CAMPUS

I love living on the Eastern campus. At a big university, I would be just a number. At Eastern, everyone knows everyone else. It's easy to meet new people, and there is so much to do. Where I'm from in Hartford, most of the people in my neighborhood are Latino or African American. It's not diverse. On our campus, it's a whole new world, with people from all over. My friend Ivan is from Norway. We talk about the political system in Norway, and we agree that the United States has to get it together. My friend Mohammed is from Egypt. Andrew is from Manchester, Connecticut, and I have another friend from Springfield, Massachusetts. I have learned that the world is larger than my home neighborhood, and it's a world that I want to get to know more.

In addition to my academics, the best thing about being at Eastern is all the opportunities that I have been given through this program. I have a job where I get to work with people; I'm the president of a student club; and I have developed some personal and professional relationships — with fellow students, with the director of career development, with the dean of students. I wouldn't be able to have these same opportunities at a bigger school.

For instance, Cliff Marrett, the director of internships and career development, has been a great mentor to me and an inspiration as well. He has taught me to be professional and to be proud of it; he also comes from Hartford. It means a lot to me to act professionally and make it, having come from the so-called slums, and then go back to my home neighborhood to educate others and show them that they can do it as well.

One of the things that they talk about at Eastern is the value of the liberal arts education that we get here and how it allows you to grow as an individual, to discover who you are. I learned that I can be a professional. I have also learned that I have the talent and ability to be a persuasive public speaker.

I realize now that I can touch people with my voice. That is my gift. That is what I've been blessed with. During my time at Eastern, I've been perfecting my public-speaking skills and have also learned how to be more professional. Knowing that I have leadership skills is humbling, because I know that I have a responsibility to use those skills to help others.

My next step is figuring out how to affect the world in a positive way. I am thinking of going to law school after I graduate so that I can advocate for the people in this world who need help the most. I really want to help make this a better world, a safer place. Many people work hard every day to do just that. Police officers, fire fighters, EMTs — they all help people. They go off to work every day, risking their lives to help people. To be able to do something positive like them — that has been my motivation to do better.

THE PURPLE TEAM

One of the things that Eastern is great about is letting students work directly with faculty and staff. It isn't like we are lowly students or second-class citizens. If a student has a good idea, the faculty and staff help you figure out how to make it happen. Kim Silcox, the director of the Center for Community Engagement, and I came up with the Purple Team Mentoring Program. Two Windham Middle School teachers had reached out to Kim and said, "We have ESL students who we are afraid are going to be lost when they graduate from middle school and go to high school. We need your help."

I worked with Kim to find other Eastern volunteers that we could bring together as a mentoring team. Once we had the team together, we went to the middle school and worked with students throughout the eighth grade, helping them get ready to transition to high school. The program has been very successful and is in its third year. Once the middle school administration saw that the program worked, it was extended to the fifth, sixth, and seventh grades so that all ESL students were served. We have about forty or fifty mentors in the middle school right now.

We are at the high school as well, with the students that we had last year who are now freshmen. We have also changed the program's name from the "Purple Team Mentors" to "Bridges to the Future."

The Bridges to the Future program is every day. Volunteers can go every day, any day they want, any time they want. We've made it more structured this year too. There are specific times when vans come, pick volunteers up, and bring them to the middle school. What we ask for is commitment and dedication. If you can come only one day per week for a specific amount of time—but you can come every week—that's all we ask. We want the kids to see who you are, what you bring to the table, and that you're here on a regular basis. That's what we ask for.

I go to the high school every Monday, Wednesday, and Friday from noon to two o'clock with four other volunteers to help the kids with their homework. They know us by now and are comfortable with us. I emphasize to the other volunteers the need to get to know the students personally. That's the best way that you can help them. I also know that once they get to high school, their issues are more personal; they have more "grown-up" issues to discuss. Boyfriends and girlfriends—you can't keep that out of the conversation. So you have to get to know your students and be on a personal level with them. The difference is you have to establish that you are a mentor, not a friend. One on hand, you have to tell them, "I've been through this before. I know what you've been through," but you are also trying to get them to find a different path. We're there to guide them and relate to them on almost every level that they've been through.

GIVING BACK HOME

Another program that I am involved in is to return to my old high school—Hartford Public High School—to talk with seniors about the importance of going to college. Kayla Bynum and I had this idea to bring other Eastern students with us back to our high school to mentor the seniors. We presented the proposal to Charlene Senteio, the guidance counselor at the high school's Law and Government Academy, as well as to Kim Silcox at Eastern. Last February, we took eight other Eastern students—six of them from Hartford—and started the program. Kayla and I have been going back to Hartford High every other Friday to help the seniors get ready for college. In the fall, we talk about filling out the financial aid forms, writing résumés, and turning in their college applications. In the spring, we talk about college—what happens once you get there. We don't sugarcoat what we say. We tell them the dos and don'ts, and we talk about specific topics that they want to discuss. They ask the typical questions—taking the SATs, financial aid, what it's like to have roommates, why we chose Eastern, and what it's like living away from home. In addition to the things that they are thinking about, we talk about the things that they need to pay attention to, like study habits, getting involved on campus, keeping themselves motivated, staying away from drugs and alcohol, and thinking about their career options. We even kick the teachers out so that we can talk openly about sensitive issues. We can be honest with them, own up to some of the things that we did in high school, and give it to them straight. They know that we are there to help them, not to lecture them like grown-ups.

A lot of the seniors are going to Eastern, so they are already familiar with us. They know us, and when they come to Eastern, we want them to be comfortable enough to be able to come to us for help. This year, I want to bring more volunteers back to Hartford and involve sophomores and juniors in the program. It's the kind of program that I would like to see in every urban high school in Connecticut.

LEADERSHIP ON CAMPUS

I really get a lot of satisfaction out of working with the Bridges program in Willimantic and going back to my old high school to talk to the kids there. But it all starts with the work that we are doing on our own campus.

Even before my freshman year, during summer orientation, my student orientation counselor told me about the MALES student club (Men Achieving Leadership, Excellence, and Success). This group teaches leadership skills to male students on campus and performs a lot of service in the local community. FEMALES (Females Excelling, Maturing to Achieve Leadership, Excellence, and Success) is our sister club.

It was another revelation. Coming from Peace Builders, doing community service, and being with at-risk students back in Hartford, I said to myself, "This is for me." There were also other MALES members at orientation, and they were very welcoming. I told them about some of the community service that I had done in Hartford, and they encouraged me to join MALES.

MALES is a big reason why I love Eastern. Even during my first few meetings in MALES, the other freshmen and I felt comfortable and welcomed by the other members. Once it came time for elections, I decided that I wanted to take the step and become the vice president of MALES, which was my role last year. When I first came to the organization, I told myself that I wanted to be president, and I ran for the office this past spring and was voted in as president for my junior year.

I am proud of some of the things that we have been able to accomplish. Last spring, we ran a leadership workshop. This year, we are hosting a public speaking workshop for other student clubs. We are working on Project Beautification with the Education Club. We also want to do more projects with other clubs, including community service with the West Indian Society, FEMALES, and the Organization of Latin American Students. In the spring, during spring break, we hope to travel somewhere to donate a week of community service to an organization or community in need. Last spring break, the MALES and FEMALES clubs went to Crosby High School in Waterbury and to Springfield Science and Technology High School in Massachusetts. We were well received in both schools and basically talked about our experiences and tried to motivate the kids there. We wanted to get them to think, "They did it, and so can I."

Being a club officer is an important role on our campus. In addition to planning and running meetings and events, you are the face of the organization; everyone sees you on campus and knows who you are. That means demonstrating professionalism and all that comes with being a leader. All the freshmen got to know me during summer orientation, so they know who I am. I'm in and out of the Student Center, so I have to keep in mind that, as a student leader on campus, I represent the student body and the university. I have a reputation to uphold in my classes and outside in the community.

MY JOB ALLOWS ME TO HELP OTHER STUDENTS

In addition to my club activities, I have an on-campus job and have had one ever since I enrolled at Eastern. It's part of the Dual College Enrollment Program model—learning responsibility, being dependable, applying the skills that I am learning on campus in a work situation. My first two years, I worked for the Center for Community Engagement. Now I am a peer counselor in the Center for Internships and Career Development. We promote the services provided by the office across the campus at what we call satellite stations—at the Academic Services Center, in Shafer Hall, at Hurley Dining Hall, and in the Student Center—where we staff tables to promote the services. We also conduct residence hall visits, stop by classrooms, and give workshop presentations to student clubs and resident assistants. Word of mouth seems to be the most effective way for us to get the word out.

I did a workshop last week in Winthrop Hall; "choosing a major" was the topic. Winthrop is the residence hall where this year's freshmen in the Dual College Enrollment Program live. I introduced myself to all the kids and exchanged phone numbers. I talked with them as a group after the workshop was over. I told them, "You are a family; you have to depend on each other." They opened up and talked about a number of things on their minds.

One girl was very shy and was worried about coming to Eastern full time next semester. At the same time, she believes that she has been successful by staying in her bubble. I encouraged her to explore the possibilities. That was the highlight of the evening. I will keep an eye on her, try to motivate her to reach out and explore, and make sure that she stays at Eastern.

I LIVE IN THREE WORLDS

When I bring my friends to campus, they are nervous. It's like they are on the street. I tell them to be cool, but it is so unfamiliar to them. I understand how they feel. I live in three worlds: I live on campus; I live in my head; and I have a life back home. I realized very early during my time at Eastern what my life on campus means—it means everything to me. But I also have an intellectual life, and I am trying to stretch my thoughts in every direction I can. Then there is my life back home. It will always be a part of me. One of my close friends died violently; he had been arrested for robberies and drugs. I try to learn from those experiences. I still have respect for my friends back home but not all that they have done. It's about balancing the two worlds of the streets and the campus. I still remember what it's like to fight to survive. It's about staying humble. It's remembering that people trust you because they can relate to you.

FAMILY SUPPORT IS IMPORTANT

My family has been very supportive of me coming to Eastern. Not only have they encouraged me going to college, but I get a lot of respect from all my family members, because I will be the only one on my mother's side of the family to have gone to college. My parents are both proud of what I am doing; I often hear them telling the rest of the family about some of the activities that I am involved in on campus. Even my uncle, whom I hadn't seen in years, got on the phone to tell me, "Do what you're doing. Keep doing it, you're making me proud."

I can't wait to see what my sister and brother—Kayla and Jordan—are going to do. I know that they are going to follow in my footsteps.

Another thing that I have done is learn to forgive my mother for divorcing my father. I love my dad and my mother, and I realize, as human beings, we're not perfect. I have learned to take all my negative energy and turn it into something positive so that I can become a better person.

I WANT TO CHANGE THE WORLD

When I first came to Eastern, I wanted to major in English, but as the year went on, I realized that wasn't what I really wanted to do. At that point, I wasn't sure what I wanted to major in; I was "undeclared." But I thought about how engaged I was at Hartford Public High's Law and Government Academy where we focused on government issues, policies, and current events. In my sophomore year at Eastern, I decided to check out political science and maybe minor in prelaw. I tried that, and it wasn't as interesting as I thought it would be. I checked out social work, and that wasn't for me either. It was a bit frustrating not finding my stride immediately. But then I took a sociology class with Professor Canterbury, and I liked that a lot. So I am majoring in sociology and minoring in prelaw. After I graduate, I intend to pursue a master's or a law degree.

Eventually, I want to go into higher education, perhaps become a professor or do something out of the ordinary. For sure, I want to be a social activist. I am not sure where I will end up, but I know I need to know more about the world. I need to travel. The first step is to go for a master's degree, maybe work at a college for a while in student affairs. Like I told my guidance counselor back at Hartford Public, my dream is to change the world in a positive way. The only way to do that is to help others and educate them. Everyone needs help sometime in their lives. I want to be that person.

* * *

Todd is on track to graduate in May 2014.

TEN

Maria Burgos-Jiménez, Class of 2012

I have become a woman who is independent, open-minded, and doesn't let obstacles or fears prevent me from doing what I want to do.

A HUMBLE LIFE IN PUÑAL

I was raised in the small town of Puñal Adentro on the outskirts of Santiago, the capital of Santiago de los Caballeros province in the Dominican Republic. I lived there through the end of seventh grade before moving to Hartford, Connecticut, with my mother and my three sisters.

When I was a child, I was very shy and reserved, and it took me a lot of time and practice to overcome my shyness. In addition to being shy, interacting with other people was also hard because my father, Hector Burgos, was and still is very strict. As a child, I was not allowed to play with my friends until my homework and chores were done. My father used to tell me that school came first before anything else because my education was the one thing that would help me to be successful in life. He also was concerned about our safety and sometimes would keep us home inside, away from the turmoil of the streets.

In Puñal, we knew everyone. We didn't have a car, and there were no buses, so I would walk both ways to school every day. It was two miles each way, but the weather was nice most of the time, so I didn't mind. I would walk with my friends Karina, Karen, and Chanel and my cousins Madeline and Yadelin.

We wore uniforms in school—a khaki skirt with a blue shirt. Looking back now, I think that the uniforms helped to bridge the social classes; everyone was treated the same way. There was no gossip about clothing, no backstabbing, no "I'm wearing a nicer dress than you"—none of that. Our school was different from schools in the United States. The classes were smaller, and we had more subjects, including culture and religion, which of course isn't taught in the public schools in America.

It was a humble life—we didn't have the financial resources and all the conveniences that we have here in the United States. Sometimes that was a good thing. We didn't have video games or watch hours of television. We would play outside most of the time—kickball was my favorite activity. I think that was healthier for us.

My father is an accountant. He got his degree at the Universidad Technológica de Santiago and was the director of accounting at a company. My dad was able to support our family on his accountant's job, so my mother didn't work outside the home. But even with his job, my father and mother realized that my sisters and I would never have the opportunity to get a good education and make something of ourselves if we stayed in the Dominican Republic.

When I was thirteen, my mother, Maria Jiménez, my three sisters, and I left Puñal and traveled to the United States to find a better way of life, coming to Hartford, where my mother's father and my aunt and uncle lived.

A QUIET GIRL IN A STRANGE LAND

My mom's father actually encouraged us to follow him to the United States, and he helped us make the arrangements. I remember the day that we arrived very clearly—it was September 17, 2003, when my mother, my sisters, and I landed in Hartford. My dad stayed in the Dominican Republic to work. In the beginning, he would send us money, but the wage scale is very different between the two countries and the exchange rate is not so good, so he couldn't help us as much as he would have liked. My two oldest sisters started working as soon as we got here to help out my mom, who had to find a job to support us. She found work at a dry-cleaning company and created a home for my sisters and me. My mother had finished high school in the Dominican Republic, but she wanted a different path for us, a better life. She has always encouraged my sisters and me to go to school and do our homework, and she made sure that we always attended class.

Coming to the United States was a shock to me on many levels. The autumn weather soon turned to winter, and I wasn't used to the cold or the snow. Everything about the culture was different—the music, clothing, food, and general lifestyle of the people around me weren't at all like what I was used to in the Dominican Republic. I had given up my life in Puñal, all the things that I was familiar with. I missed my friends, and I was all alone in middle school; my two sisters were together in high school.

I started the eighth grade at South Middle School. I had no friends to depend on, but I was determined to overcome any obstacles that I found. I knew that it was going to be difficult. It wasn't that I was afraid, but I wasn't always sure how I was being received, how well the teachers and other students understood my limited English, and how they perceived me as someone from a different culture. Sometimes I would hear someone say, "She has an accent," and I would stop talking entirely.

The most difficult challenge that I faced was clearly the language barrier—I couldn't speak or understand more than a few words of English—basically I could say, "Hi," and that was about it. When I got to Hartford High School, I was placed in bilingual and ESL programs for three years. Most of the time, both English and Spanish were spoken in class, and I also had an English class just to focus on learning the language. Going back and forth from one language to the other was confusing at first, but it helped me interact with other Latino students who were facing the same situation.

One particular challenge was when the books were in English but the language being spoken in class was Spanish. To do my homework, I had to read the English lessons with a dictionary and translate the words into Spanish so that I could understand the topic well enough to answer the questions in English.

It was also very hard to go to school to learn English and then come home to speak only Spanish with my mother. My sisters were also learning the language, and they helped me to pronounce certain words and to understand how some words were used differently depending on the situation.

Another thing that people don't always realize is that while Spanish is spoken throughout Latin America, every country has its different dialects and vocabulary. Most of the Latinos in Hartford are Puerto Ricans and Mexicans. Learning English is a challenge for all of us, but we come at it from different starting points.

I think that this time in my life—at the beginning of my teenage years—was the hardest time for someone to move to a new country. Younger children seem to make friends easily, and adults are more settled in who they are. I had left all my friends in Puñal just at the time that I was starting to grow up. Leaving those friendships and those feelings of comfort and familiarity behind, I came to a big city without having any friends, without being able to speak the language, and with my own natural shyness to contend with. Thankfully, I had my family with me for support.

MY GREATEST INSPIRATION

My mom is my greatest inspiration. She gave up everything for us when we came to the United States. It was very hard on her to travel to a new country alone with her four daughters, with only a high school education, unable to speak the language, and without her husband by her side to support her. She has struggled a lot so that we could have a better life, and she has worked hard so that my sisters and I could focus on our schoolwork. My mother still works at the same dry cleaners that she started at in 2003, and she still doesn't speak English very well; she understands just enough of what is said to get by.

Without my mom, I would have gone down a different path. All around us in Hartford, you could see the typical things that kids in the city get involved with—drugs, delinquency, violence, unmarried pregnancies. But we were lucky; we didn't get into trouble. My mom helped us stay away from those things. She has always been there to support us, and as I have grown up, I now understand how hard she has worked for us. I went to high school with so many kids who didn't see a better future for themselves. Some of my friends didn't finish high school, let alone go to college. They got married, and some had children without getting married. One of my classmates had her third child as I was finishing my senior year at Hartford Public High School.

DAD WAS ALWAYS HERE IN MY HEART

Even though my father stayed in the Dominican Republic to work, he was always here in my heart. He would call me on the phone frequently and give me guidance. I would tell him what was happening in my life, and even though he wasn't with us in person, we had great conversations. If I wasn't sure of something, he would counsel me. I felt that our bond was still there, even though he wasn't living with us all the time. He would tell me, "Don't be afraid of doing what you want to do. Take advantage of the opportunities that are given to you when you are young."

My dad finally came to the United States in 2009, and my parents bought a house on New Britain Avenue in Hartford. My father still doesn't understand or speak English very well, and he can't work as an accountant here. He has a job at Home Goods, the home decorations store. It's just nice to finally have him here with us.

MORE SUPPORT IN HIGH SCHOOL

Once I got to Hartford Public High School, things got easier. I had my sisters there as role models, and I was finally learning the English language. By my senior year, all of my classes were in English. Denisse, Rossio, and I all looked up to my older sister Diosmedy, who was already in college. The three of us wanted to follow her and have a career.

Hartford Public High School wasn't as rigorous when I was there as it is now. The instruction for English-language learners has improved a lot. The transitional classes didn't advance my English skills as quickly as they do now, but fortunately, many of my teachers gave me extra help.

Mr. Felix was my ninth-grade math teacher, and he was a huge influence on me. He would give me advice on how to get involved in student organizations. He pushed me to keep up my grades. He told me the importance of taking the right math classes to prepare for college, and he encouraged me to learn more about what college was like. He would counsel me when I was struggling, and he'd push me to do better when he felt I wasn't trying hard enough. "When you fall, you need to get up and continue," he would tell me. I worked hard and ended up being twelfth in my graduating class of more than two hundred students.

I had other supporters at Hartford Public High School. Maria Pastorelli was my guidance counselor. She was very passionate about our success—"Did you write your essay?" "Did you finish your application?" She was like a big sister, helping me step-by-step through the college application process. Maria is an alumna of St. Joseph's College in Hartford, and she wanted me to go there. It is close to where I live, so I applied, and she took me to its campus for a tour. It's a good school, and I got accepted. But it is a private college, and it wasn't able to give me enough financial aid for me to attend—the cost was still out of my family's reach.

AT EASTERN'S DOORSTEP

I actually visited Eastern as a junior and applied there in addition to applying to St. Joseph's. Because my English writing skills were still shaky, the people at Eastern told me that I would have to complete a summer enrichment program to prove I was ready to enroll.

Maria then told me about Eastern's Dual College Enrollment Program. She explained that I would have to take some courses at Quinebaug Valley Community College for a semester and then transition to Eastern. Unfortunately, I was late finding out about the program, and it had already made its selections for the first group of students. However, Mr. Bartlett, our college specialist, didn't give up, and he convinced the people at Eastern to come back to interview me. Kimberly Crone, the director of admissions, talked with me and decided to add me to the group—so I got in after all!

Initially, I didn't like the idea of going to the community college, but Maria convinced me that it would give me time to improve my English and acquire more academic skills. I realized that it was a first step and good preparation for enrolling full-time at Eastern.

THE HUMAN MIND

I remember clearly the day that I decided that I wanted to go to college to study psychology. In my sophomore year at Hartford Public High School, my law class teacher was talking about how the brain functions and why people do what they do. She had a law background but was also a psychologist. I was curious about what psychologists did. When my mother took me to the doctor's, I realized that I liked the science of medicine. I began to understand that psychology is a field in the world of medicine, and I realized that I wanted to learn how the human mind works and how people socialize.

FRESHMAN YEAR

In my first semester, I took an economics class at Eastern and math, writing, and reading classes at Quinebaug Valley Community College. At first, I was intimidated by just the thought of going to college, especially the idea of living on campus away from home. Attending Eastern turned out not to be as big and as intimidating a transition as I expected. I was worried that I wasn't going to have the same level of support that I experienced at Quinebaug. I was wrong. Eastern professors are very warm and are always willing to give you extra help—they want to make connections with their students.

My first professor at Eastern was Maryanne Clifford in economics. I remember when I took her course that she made class a lot of fun. One day, I was doing a project and didn't understand something, and I was afraid to go see her. But when I went to her office, she was great. I learned that day that sometimes you just need to take that first step; don't be afraid to show your emotions or your struggles.

Even while I was taking English and other remedial courses at Quinebaug Valley Community College, I was living in the dorms at Eastern. In freshman year, I lived in Burr Hall, which is the oldest building on campus. When I first came to Burr, I was homesick. I missed my family, even though they were just forty-five minutes away. It was the first time that I had been away from my mother, and I was the first sister to live on a college campus; Rossio and Diosmedy had commuted to Central, and Dennisse had even commuted to UConn, which is thirty-five miles from our home.

I would stay in my room alone while my roommate went out. After about two weeks, they switched my roommate, and Keila Collado, another student in the Dual College Enrollment Program, joined me. We both were from Hartford Public High School, but I didn't know her then. We came to be very good friends. It seems funny that we didn't even speak to each other when we were in high school, but once we got to Eastern, she became one of my best friends. We were roommates for three years before she got married and moved to California.

Burr Hall ended up being a lot of fun. It was like a little family—I knew some of the other students from Hartford High, and we had a lot of social events to help us get to know one another. Slowly, I let go of my shyness, and I discovered the many social activities and support services available on campus.

In my second semester, I enrolled full-time at Eastern. I took a social psychology class with Professor Cousins about how people socialize, how we behave around other people. I also took a class with Dr. Margaret Letterman. She is amazing! She engages every student in the subject matter and is so enthusiastic about the work that she does. Dr. Letterman was my adviser for the Organization for Latin American Students. She also sponsors dinners on Thursdays when students from all kinds of cultures and backgrounds get together to eat and socialize. From the very beginning, I had a connection with her. I would visit Dr. Letterman often to get her advice or ask a question about something. She would encourage me to send her my papers to look at before I handed them in—and not just for her own classes. She also helped me get my internship at Sweeney Elementary School.

HAVING MY FAMILY TO LEAN ON

I am the youngest of four sisters, and we are all very close. My oldest sister, Diosmedy, is six years older than I am, and she had started college in the Dominican Republic when we left to come to the United States. She also had challenges with the English language when we came to America. She eventually graduated from Central Connecticut State University and now works at IBM as an accountant—just like my dad! She also just got married. Rossio is the second oldest and is studying political science, also at Central. My third sister is Denisse. She graduated from the University of Connecticut with a degree in biology and wants to study at Quinnipiac University to become a physician's assistant.

Having the opportunity to speak to my other family members about my college experience has been invaluable. My dad and my older sisters can tell me what their experiences were like in college: "This is how you do it." Even though my mom didn't go to college, she has always been very supportive—"You need to do this!" It's not just the prior family experience in college that has meant so much to me; it's all the positive support. We talk about it all the time—"This is the path you must take." "Think about the difference in your life if you do."

Many of my friends' parents didn't go to college. I can help them now by explaining how to apply to college, how to apply for financial aid. Even visiting a school is a big deal—some of my friends were too timid or frightened to visit a college. They were resigned to going to a community college, limiting their vision to going to college for two years. I don't think people realize how big these barriers are—the lack of support, resources, and family history. I have been very fortunate.

NEW FRIENDS TO ENJOY LIFE WITH

As I got comfortable in my new environment, I made new friends. Maiyah Gamble-Rivers was the girl who lived in the room next to me. She's from Providence, Rhode Island. We didn't connect immediately; I didn't think she liked me. We started to talk and became best friends. We took classes together; we ate together in Hurley Dining Hall; and we went to movies together. Maiyah also got me interested in doing community service with her. We participated in Town Wide/Town Pride, the downtown beautification project that Eastern students conduct each spring; we tutored at the local middle school and high school; and we volunteered for the Walk for Warmth for Windham Area Interfaith Ministry. I also volunteered at the Women's Center and participated in the American Cancer Society's Relay for Life.

Maiyah and I did all the things that friends do, but we also helped each other grow academically and socially. She would also proofread my papers before I handed them in. She was always there to help me. Maiyah is in Washington, DC, now. She has always been interested in art and how to nurture creativity in children, and she wants to build a career in that field.

BLOSSOMING AT EASTERN

I am very grateful for the friends that I have met at Eastern—and not just my student friends.

The program coordinator was like my second mom. Whether it was a personal or academic issue, she was always there for me. If I was struggling in a class, she would call and encourage me. She would say, "Check out these resources." She would give me advice. Having her there made me feel like I was at home. I also received several scholarships from the Eastern Connecticut State University Foundation, which helped my family and me to pay for tuition and books.

Not every student who goes to college gets the support that I did. I know that I would not have finished college in four years without it. Of course, not every class I took was pleasant. My art history class was the class that I liked the least. At one point, I thought of dropping it. I didn't feel that I was learning enough. I felt that if I was paying for the course, I needed to do well and feel like I was getting something out of it. But I stuck with it and challenged myself.

I am proud of the fact that I never dropped a class in four years. I just figured, if I drop a class, I will have to take it at some point anyway, maybe with the same professor. It was simply delaying the inevitable. I realized that sticking it out would help me grow and mature and give me a better perspective. I have found that it is better to work hard and be challenged—you learn more and grow more that way. It's better not to get too comfortable in life.

WORKING ON CAMPUS

During my time at Eastern, I worked for several different departments, and each experience helped direct my career choice or helped me grow in some other way. When I first decided to work at the child care center with kids, I was debating whether I wanted to be a child psychologist or work with adults. At the center, I learned about children's behaviors and how children develop at different ages. That experience made me realize that I definitely wanted to work in the field of child psychology. I had the opportunity to learn how to relate to little ones, to build trust with a child. If you don't know how to speak to children and create a bond with them, you will not be able to help them when they are having difficulties. Sometimes, one of the kids didn't want to take a nap, and I had to help him or her. Without a nap, children are cranky. I had to find a way to help them sleep.

I also worked in the Admissions Office for Kim Crone, who had initially interviewed me when I was applying to the Dual College Enrollment Program. Of course, when I interviewed for the program, I didn't realize that she was going to end up being my supervisor. I was surprised to see her, but I developed a very strong bond with her. As a tour guide in the Admissions Office, I had the opportunity to tell prospective students about our campus. I had to become an expert about the campus and all the resources available to students. It felt good telling other students about the value of attending a small liberal arts college.

I will never forget one day in 2010, when I was going back to Eastern from my home in Hartford. My sister Denisse was bringing me back to campus to take an exam, and her car broke down. Her Triple A membership had expired, so I was walking up the road trying to call my other sister, but she was at work. I was trying to figure out whom else to call and was getting pretty frantic about missing my exam. As I was walking down the road, Kim Crone drove by the other way heading to Hartford for a meeting. She thought that I was all alone, because Denisse had stayed in the car. Kim turned around, missed her appointment, and drove me back to campus for me to take my exam. She literally kept me from failing the course. She missed a meeting to help me out. How can I ever forget that?

APPLYING MY KNOWLEDGE

At Eastern, they say that students get a "liberal education, practically applied." I was very fortunate to apply my own psychology coursework directly in an elementary school setting. I worked as an intern at Sweeney Elementary School in Willimantic for an entire school year, working for a classroom teacher as well as the school psychologist, Mr. Goldberg. Working with the classroom teacher, I was able to assist students academically while contributing to the management of pupil behavior. I learned different teaching methods and learning styles. The teacher let me teach the class with her. I worked in two different grades with four to six kids at a time, students who had disabilities or behavioral problems. Some had speech delays; others had language issues. Most of them were Latino—Puerto Ricans, Guatemalans, and Mexicans.

I worked with bilingual students and helped them to interpret their dialect, translate it into English, and learn a new vocabulary by translating Spanish into English sentences. I remember one time when I tried to explain something to a student in Spanish, and he got so confused he started crying. I told him, "It's okay that you don't understand this. You just need to keep at it." I was able to relate my own experiences to him. Also, when I tutored math and the students didn't understand the problem, I would rework the issue and find another way for them to comprehend it. I might use Spanish to explain it if English didn't work. Even though it was math, they were more comfortable hearing about it in Spanish.

I also assisted Mr. Goldberg in collecting data of behavioral assessments, primarily through conducting direct classroom observations of individual students, comparing kids with disabilities to students who were functioning normally. I was allowed to sit in on placement and planning team meetings with the psychologist, teachers, and parents to discuss how to address the children's behavior and improve their academic performance. It was very interesting, and I was able to give my own opinions and analysis, offering ideas on how and what could be done better.

A DREAM COME TRUE

I like to explore the world on the Internet. When I saw photos of Florence, Italy, I wanted to visit there. How I got there is a funny story. Maiyah and I decided to play a game. Each of us wrote down the names of three

European countries that we wanted to visit—I wrote down Spain, Italy, and France. We both had written "Italy," so we decided to go there. My advisor helped me plan the trip, and the university gave me a grant from a fund that it has set up to help students afford to study abroad.

Maiyah and I landed in Florence on January 25, 2011. For the first two weeks, I was homesick. Even though Maiyah was with me, I missed my mom and my sisters. It was like 2003 all over again—starting off in a new country. But I told myself, "I've done this once; I can do it again." And I did.

It was the most amazing experience that I have ever had in my life. It was so different from my experiences in either Puñal or Willimantic that it almost felt like a fantasy. It really was a dream come true. I took five classes at the Lorenzo de' Medici, the Italian International Institute: four classes related to my psychology major and a class in Italian. We also had time to travel to other cities in Italy and other countries; I visited Venice, Rome, Pisa, Tuscany, Paris, and London. Going with Maiyah made the experience that much more meaningful. It was an opportunity to learn about new people, food, and music. I also met students from around the United States as well as students from other European countries. Interestingly, there were no students at the school from Italy. I would have enjoyed going to school with students from the country we were visiting.

I am Catholic, and visiting the Vatican in Rome was an inspiration. My mom had said that she always wanted to go there, so I called her on Skype and told her about all the things I saw. It was my way of sharing the experience with her. I also took a lot of photos and shared them with my family and friends.

Visiting the mausoleum of Pope Paul II was truly special. I also visited St. Peter's Square, St. Paul's Basilica, the Statue of David, and the Colosseum. I threw a coin in Trevi Fountain. I discovered that the churches in Italy are truly art treasures, and I enjoyed learning about their history. Even the bridges, like Ponte Vecchio in Florence, are works of art.

Studying and traveling in Europe has affected my life in many different ways. I have now had the opportunity to experience and live in three different cultures. It helps me appreciate the life that I have, and it makes me even more grateful for my family. I also learned some Italian. That was an interesting experience. It felt very much like the same process of learning a new language and a new culture that I had experienced coming to the United States in 2003. The difference is that I had my friend with me, as well as other students in Florence who spoke English like I did. I found that it was easier to integrate into the culture there. Perhaps it was also because Italian and Spanish are similar.

GRADUATION DAY

My graduation was like going back to the Dominican Republic. My parents, my sisters, and my cousins from Puñal all came. Having them there for me, feeling their support throughout my journey to get to and through college was truly special. After the graduation ceremony, we went out to dinner. Denisse had graduated a week before me, so it was an especially warm and happy time for my family.

THANK YOU!

I want to thank Dr. Núñez for founding the Dual College Enrollment Program. Eastern has given me many things—the chance to meet new friends and invaluable mentors who helped me throughout my four years of college and, most important, the opportunity to grow as an individual and to accomplish many of my dreams.

WHAT'S NEXT?

Since graduating from Eastern in May 2012, I have focused on working in my field and preparing for graduate school. I have been working part-time at Classical Magnet School as a tutor and as the assistant to the enrichment program director.

I am also volunteering at Hartford Hospital as a research assistant in the emergency room. I have worked on several studies, including one about patients trying to quit smoking and a study of elderly and others who are at risk of falling down.

I have recently been studying for the GREs, which I will be taking in February. I have been thinking about a graduate program that combines business and clinical psychology, and I am looking into programs at Boston College, the University of Chicago, and the University of North Carolina. I want to get my master's degree and my doctorate and then work in a hospital or a private clinic with children and adults with disabilities, autism, and behavioral issues. I want to give back in the way that people have given me opportunities. There are so many children and adults going through tough times. I want to give them support and the chance for a better life.

ELEVEN

Eshwar Gulcharran

I have to do what I have made my mind up to do.

LIVING THE SIMPLE LIFE

I was born in Guyana and lived there for the first eight years of my life. Guyana is on the northeast coast of South America, east of Venezuela and north of Brazil. The name "Guyana" is the native word in my country for "the land of many waters." In addition to the Atlantic Ocean to the north, Guyana has many rivers. Much of the land along the coast is below sea level and full of swamps and sandbars. There are miles and miles of canals and ditches, bordered by dams and dikes, to keep the towns from flooding. The houses are built on stilts or pilings, and it rains much of the time. As you travel inland from the coast, the many rivers lead away into the wet rainforest.

My family lived in New Amsterdam at one point, but for most of the time we lived in Georgetown in the same house, made of wood and up on stilts to protect against flooding. We lived about two hours by foot from the ocean. I remember one time I was on my bike coming home from school, and it started raining. By the time I got to my house, the water was up to my waist. It was like that often.

It was a simple life—we didn't need much electricity, didn't have a phone, and didn't have a television until I was six or seven years old. It was summer all the time, so there was no snow, no need for a furnace or a fireplace to stay warm.

Growing up in Guyana was fun; it is always hot there, so my friends and I spent most of the time outside playing cricket. Since coming to the United States, I have learned to play a variety of sports, including baseball, which doesn't interest me as much. I have always liked cricket more.

133

It's just different and more exciting to me. There are two "home plates," called "stumps" or "wickets," not just one. The bat touches the ground as you wait for the ball to be pitched. And you have to get all eleven players on the other team out before your team can bat. You make outs by having the ball caught, when the "bowler" knocks over the wicket, or if you hit the ball and a fielder is able to knock the wicket off before you can reach the other wicket. You have to play the game to really get a feel for it, but it's played all over the world, and I love it.

Living near the rainforest and the jungle, we really didn't need a car. We could walk to wherever we needed to go. It was not a life based on technology. We had a vegetable garden in our backyard, and we raised much of our food. I remember having guava and cherry trees in the yard as well. We also had chickens. Life was simpler—we would gather our food during the day, cook it, and eat it: as simple as that.

My mother's name is Leonie; she has both Indian and Caucasian heritage and is Catholic. My father, Moneshwar, is Hindu. Guyana was first colonized by the Dutch, who brought African slaves to the country to work. After the English took over control of Guyana in the nineteenth century, they brought people from India to work in the sugarcane and rice fields. That is how my father's ancestors came from India to Guyana.

The language spoken in Guyana is called "Creolese," which is a dialect of English influenced by all the people who have come to live in my country—the native tribes, the Dutch, people from Africa, people from India, and the British.

My mother didn't finish high school, and the furthest that my father got was middle school. He has always been a really hard worker, doing what he has to do to take care of our family. He's good with his hands and has a lot of street smarts and common sense. I respect my father because he is true to his family and himself.

In Guyana, my father worked in the sugarcane and rice fields and did odd jobs. Sometimes he and I would go fishing on the dams. We didn't need a boat, and there were always lots of different types of fish to catch—freshwater fish. We would bring them home, clean them, and cook them. You didn't have to go to a grocery store; the food you ate wasn't packaged up in plastic; and there were no preservatives or chemicals. You ate what you gathered; you lived off the land. We would catch fish or gather vegetables from our own garden, maybe kill a chicken. Cook that, relax, and enjoy the rest of the day. Then we would do the same thing again the next day.

Curry was one of my favorite dishes, and we made the traditional "garam masala" curry powder from a blend of cumin, cardamom, peppercorn, cloves, and other spices. We also had ginger, cinnamon, and tamarinds—so many flavors and tastes to choose from. My mom did most of the cooking, but my dad also likes to cook, sometimes even better than my mom!

In the jungles of Guyana, you can find all species of wild animals—jaguars, tapirs, anteaters, anacondas, and of course, the trees are full of monkeys. One time, my dad caught a monkey and brought him home and put him in our guava tree. He stayed around for a while, but he was trouble. We finally released him back into the jungle.

A BETTER LIFE BECKONS

As a kid, I was having a great time living in Guyana, and I went to primary school through the third grade. Within each grade in elementary school, you progressed up through the levels—level 1, level 2—based on test scores. I remember it as a good life, but my father worked most of the time, and I think that my parents always had moving to the United States in the back of their minds.

My grandfather's brother had come to the New York City area in 1942. My mother's grandparents had also moved to the states. They were the ones who encouraged us to move here.

At some point, my parents decided that they wanted a better life for themselves and for me, so we came to the United States right before my ninth birthday, in 2000. We landed in Queens, New York, where my mother's aunts and uncles live.

When you first come to a new country, nothing is settled. My father was checking out all his options, trying to get comfortable, trying to get situated. His cousins lived in Connecticut, and so we came to Hartford. I remember going to a doctor's office on my ninth birthday for a chicken-pox vaccine so that I could go to school there.

I started out in the fifth grade. They held me back a grade, which was a drag, but my American English wasn't very good; it took me about a year to pick it up. And then we moved back to New York. Over the years, we would move back and forth from Queens to Hartford a number of times. My mother's family was in New York, which has a lot going on and was very multicultural and more familiar to us, while my father's family was in Hartford. In New York, we lived in a basement apartment much of the time, and my dad worked two jobs—night shifts, whatever he had to do. My mom worked as a nurse's aide helping elderly people in their homes.

My grandfather—my mom's dad—is a writer, and I enjoy talking with him about all kinds of things. My dad's mother has a visa, so she frequently comes and goes from Guyana to the states; I get to see her quite a bit as well.

My younger brother was born a year after we got to the states. All the men in my family have Eshwar in their names. My dad is Moneshwar; his brother has Eshwar in his name; and my brother's name is Bhunesh-

war. Eshwar means "God" in Hindi; it's another name for the Hindu god
Shiva.

GETTING USED TO A NEW COUNTRY

Getting used to a new culture involves a lot of changes. Some of them
you just don't think about until you have to deal with them. Of course,
the cold weather and snow were a shock that I still can't say that I am
crazy about; in Guyana, it's always summer.

I also had to learn American English when I got here, but it wasn't as
big a deal as it is for my friends who are Hispanic. They still speak mostly
Spanish in their homes, and I know that learning English has been a
struggle for them.

One of the biggest things that I have had to get used to is the food in
America. In Guyana, we ate a lot of spicy foods, but the food was fresh —
fresh fish, raw vegetables and fruits, crabs and other seafood, freshly
killed chickens. In the United States, everything is processed, treated
with chemicals, packaged, and shipped to a grocery store. It takes a long
time for your stomach to get used to those changes. Pizza was something
that it took a while for me to like. Now I really enjoy Italian food and
Chinese food, but we still like to cook with the ingredients that we had in
Guyana. You can find some of those spices and other foods in Queens,
which is why my family still likes to go down there sometimes just to
shop.

Your stomach does change over time. I went back to visit our family in
Guyana in June 2009 for two weeks. What surprised me the most was
that I couldn't eat the food right off; my stomach had gotten used to the
food in the states. I couldn't eat the curry or the roti. The crabs and
seafood made me sick. It took me the entire time, but by the end of two
weeks, I had my appetite back and was able to eat some of the Guyanese
food. I guess I am an American now!

BACK AND FORTH, BACK AND FORTH

I am proud of how hard I have worked on my English-language skills. I
am told that I have no accent today. Even in high school during my
sophomore year, I remember that a girl came up to me and asked if I was
Guyanese. I said yes. She said, "You don't sound like Guyanese; you
sound like you speak fluent English."

That didn't just happen. I had a teacher who would sit and work with
me just on my English lessons. But for the most part, I learned English on
my own during middle school when we lived in New York.

It was a good time for me. I learned to play handball, hung out with
my friends, and had a chance just to be a kid. I started high school in

Queens with the same friends I had in middle school. Then things turned upside down when I moved to Hartford Public High School for my sophomore year. I had to make new friends at the same time that I was dealing with family issues.

I went to two different high schools during those years. I went to Richmond Hill High in Queens in my freshman and junior years, and then I went to Hartford Public High School in my sophomore and senior years. It was difficult to stay in contact with my friends, what with moving back and forth, and I also was dealing with my parents' relationship, which has been rocky at times. Sometimes I was pretty much living by myself.

In my junior year, my parents were still having issues. I told them that I had to leave. By then, I was nineteen. They were mature adults, and I told them to handle it themselves; I was tired of being in the middle of it. So I went back to New York to live with my aunt and cousin. I still had friends there, and my girlfriend lived nearby in Queens as well; she helped me a lot during that time.

Even so, I felt that coming back to Hartford Public High School for my senior year was good for me. I think that I got a better education there than at Richmond Hill in New York. For one thing, at Hartford Public, I was in the new Law and Government Academy, and we had to wear a dress shirt and tie every day. It made me look and feel more professional and serious about school. It helped change my attitude and made me look at myself differently—I had more potential than perhaps I had realized.

I was fortunate that I didn't get into a lot of trouble in high school. But no one is perfect. One time as a freshman in Queens, a group of my friends and I decided to skip school, so we hopped on the subway and went to Manhattan. As soon as we got up to the street level, we ran into a group of police officers. At that time of day, it was obvious that we were skipping school. I had to produce my ID, and they ended up taking us to a police station in lower Manhattan for four hours. When my mom and my uncle came to get me, I got the point. You have to learn from everything you do, and that was a lesson that stuck with me—do the right thing.

GETTING INTO EASTERN

A lot of people have helped me since I have been at Eastern, but the person that I owe the most to getting here is my friend May Ryan. She was an after-school director at Hartford Public High School, and then she went to Eastern. After she graduated, she came back to Hartford High and was the director of a program called "High Hopes," an after-school program to help kids stay out of trouble. We could socialize, dance to music, hang out with our friends, get help with homework, and enjoy different recreational activities.

One day when I was in my senior year, I was talking to May about college. I wanted to go, but I wasn't sure how to do it, what schools to apply to, what to look for. She said that Eastern was a good school, so I checked it out and applied, but it didn't accept me at first. I also applied to the University of Connecticut and Southern Connecticut State University, but I didn't get in to either of them. May told me about the Dual College Enrollment Program at Eastern, and I looked into it further. I took a writing assessment, which went okay, and a math assessment, which went even better. I was also interviewed by a team of people from Eastern—Dr. Indira Petoskey; Ismael Gracia, a student in the program who had also graduated from Hartford Public; Chris Dorsey, the admissions director; and José Aponte, who is at Quinebaug Valley Community College's Willimantic Center. They wanted to know what I wanted to do with my life and why they should select me. I told them, "If I get the opportunity to do this, I'll do it to the best of my abilities."

If I hadn't ended up at Eastern, I am not sure what would have happened to me. I might have tried to commute to community college, but I wouldn't have liked that because I really needed to get out of the house. Certainly, if I had stayed home to help out financially, things would be easier for my dad. But I made a decision that I know was the right one, because I can now see myself with a future. But it's still difficult. It's hard to balance things, because I want to help my father, to put less stress on him.

Being on my own, getting to know a whole new set of people my own age, people with some of the same intellectual interests that I have, has been a whole new experience for me, totally different from what I expected. And I never thought that I would be the first one to go to college from my family. But I have to do what I have made up my mind to do.

THE PRESSURES OF HOME

Not everyone in my family is happy about me going to college, at least not to my face. From the beginning, my dad was upset. He didn't want me to attend college, because he felt like I needed to help out at home. He wanted me to work and help out financially, to give him an extra hand around the house. I told him, "Dad, I have an opportunity here, I'm not going to waste it. I'm a young man now, and I can make my own decisions." So I decided to come to Eastern despite his feelings. He still calls me and says he misses me.

My mom is the same way. She called me yesterday and was saying, "How come you don't call home?" She was upset, and I had to explain that I am busy here at school. Life is too short to let things go to waste, so I try to stay busy doing the things I have to do.

My parents don't tell me that they're happy about me going to college, but I hear it from my aunt because my mom talks to her and I talk to my aunt. So I know how they really feel; they just can't say it to me directly. My aunt will tell me, "When you aren't home, your mom cries, but they are tears of joy." My mom just won't do it in front of me.

Growing up, I never really had that emotional connection with my parents, but being more mature now, I feel more connected with them now than I did. I understand how they manage their emotions. So even though I don't see their happiness with me, I know they have it. When I find out through my aunt and others—that makes me feel better.

THE COLLEGE LIFE

My first semester in college was a very positive experience for me. The people at Quinebaug Valley Community College were very helpful. José Aponte was great. Not only do he and the other staff there make you feel welcomed, but they were always checking in on me—"How are you doing? Is there anything you need?" The teachers helped me with my papers, and I got to meet a lot of nice people. Quinebaug's main campus is in Danielson, so the Willimantic space is small, but they were very good to me, and it's just down the hill from Eastern.

From day one, I enjoyed living on Eastern's campus. It's beautiful. I had my own room for most of the time because my roommate had moved out. It was a whole new environment—totally different from Queens or the south end of Hartford, and I felt like an explorer. There is always something to do on campus and lots of services and people to help you, so I spent some time figuring how everything works and what my choices were. All the students on campus, not just those of us in the Dual College Enrollment Program, are encouraged to use the resources on campus. The Academic Services Center, the Advising Center, the Financial Aid Office—the people are always willing to help, and it always seems like I get my questions answered or get help on my schoolwork when I go to any of those services.

I also joined the billiards club just to meet some new people and relax in the Student Center when I wasn't in class. And I joined MALES (Men Achieving Leadership, Excellence, and Success), a student club that promotes leadership skills in male students and performs a lot of service projects in the community. Todd Aviles, the vice president in my freshman year, is now the president, and over the past summer we got to know each other again. I knew him in high school but not real well, and now he's like a brother to me.

Maybe my biggest step is my job this year. In my freshman year, I worked in the Intercultural Center as an office assistant. This year, I'm a resident assistant (RA) in Niejadlik Hall; it's a lot of responsibility. I have sophomores and juniors in our dorm. I am responsible for the whole floor, and I also take turns with other RAs to staff the front desk for the entire residence hall.

One of things that we are encouraged to do is to help the students deal with their issues. It's important for them to know that someone cares about what is going on in their daily lives. I can connect with them on a personal level and listen to their stories. I feel like I am here on this Earth to help people, so that is what I try to do as an RA.

I try to learn as much as I can from the other staff in the housing office. They give me great advice on how to do programming—people like Luz Burgos, the hall director for Burnap Hall and my mentor in the student leadership program. I recently sponsored a social reception for all the kids in our dorm. It lasted three hours, and thirty-seven students came. I bought pizza, popcorn, beverages and arranged for music, and we all watched the Giants football game. We had a great time!

I am also on the Resident Assistant Council, and we are planning some activities just for RAs—a movie night, an ugly sweater party—fun things to do so that the RAs can be a stronger team and take that energy back to their halls. Next month, we are going to New York to see the sights in Manhattan.

There are a lot of things to learn in this job, and it's all helping me develop more in my own life and get to where I need to be. I see myself growing in all kinds of ways. I am more mature, more responsible. I cut my hair shorter, and I dress more professionally. I have a broader perspective on the world as well.

I have also pledged to the Lambda Alpha Upsilon fraternity, which was established in 1985 for college students of Latin American descent and is now a multicultural fraternity. We don't have fraternities at Eastern, so I go up to the Xi Chapter at the University of Connecticut to participate. Two weeks ago, we participated in the Breast Cancer Walk. I get to meet new people who share my interests, and it's another way to expand my network. I love our motto—"You are your brother's keeper." I want to stay true to that belief, and I value it a great deal. If I can have those connections and those relationships throughout my life, I will be happy.

EVERYONE NEEDS A TEAM

Luz Burgos has been an amazing supporter for me. She has really helped me learn the ropes as an RA. She cooks for me; she motivates me to keep my grades up; and she helps me plan my class schedule. She's been great.

Michael Pina, who is in MALES, helped me pledge to the fraternity. I have met all these other students—like Todd Aviles and Derwin Hill—who have become my personal network. From living pretty much on my own in New York back in high school to having this group of friends is special; I know that a lot of students can't say that they have this much support and these many resources. I feel blessed.

My professors are great too. Professor Switchenko is so funny. I am taking applied anatomy and physiology with him, and he manages to make everything interesting. I am truly excited about his class. He makes it really simple—he says that he is there to help us get ahead, to help us establish our careers.

I also like having chats with Professor Stocker, with whom I am taking an introductory philosophy course. We talk about big ideas like "free will" and other philosophical concepts. Next semester, I am taking a science course and a movie appreciation class, as well as English over the winter break. Astronomy is also something I hope to take before I am done.

In my freshman year, I had a wonderful class in improvisational theatre. The professor was very energetic and always in a good mood. I am not that good in the morning, but she made it fun. We learned to express our own unique personalities through a series of theatrical movements and skits. It was a chance to focus on performance, not just on reading or writing. I learned how to project my voice in a public speaking situation. I also attended a lecture by the actor Dan Lauria from *Wonder Years*, and he showed movie clips of how movies were made in the old days with only one camera. It was a whole new perspective on how movies are made now; I think I like the old ways better. We also watched plays on campus, and I took a date to the Hartford Stage. It made me realize that the theater is a cool place.

FRIENDS BACK HOME

I try to stay in touch with both my friends in New York and my friends in Hartford. It gets harder to maintain those relationships over time, but it's important to me. I have two totally different sets of friends, in addition to those I have here at Eastern, and it is interesting to see how much where you live influences what you do in your life.

I have a lot of opportunities to share my experiences at Eastern with my friends back home—on Facebook, calling them, texting them. We still keep in touch and talk. They always ask me what I am doing because nobody really expected me to go to college, including myself. So when my friends and I talk, I am proud to tell them about what I am doing at the university; I am proud of the success that I am having. I think that they are impressed, at least I hope that they see me as a role model for what they can do in their own lives.

I talk with my friends about what Eastern has done for me, and I tell them that I want them to go to college too. I even tell my cousins who just graduated high school, "I want you to be where I'm at in the next two years or three years. Go to college and get an education; make your life how you want it."

At the same time, I don't want them to look at me as if I think I'm a big shot or that I am going to college and they aren't. My friends don't look at me like that. Some of them are going to community college; a couple of them, like Blair and Todd from my high school, are also at Eastern.

REACHING DOWN TO LIFT UP

My little brother Bhuneshwar is ten. I feel like he's my own kid in a way. When he calls me, I ask him how he is doing in school, how are his grades, has he made new friends—those kinds of things. My father tells me that when I am not home, Bhuneshwar says that he wants to grow up to be like me. He never says it to me, but I understand. That's how my family is. People in my family tend to keep their emotions to themselves. But I know he's proud of me and sees me as a role model. If he ever does want to talk about college and his future, I'm here for him. I want to give him guidance so that he has a clearer path to go down, so he doesn't have so many obstacles in the way.

DAD, I WANT A BARBEQUE

Today, my dad drives a forklift at Data Mail in Newington, working hard for our family as usual. Two years ago, he was able to buy a house on Madison Avenue in Hartford. It all started when we were living in New York eight years ago in a basement apartment. It was really bad; my dad didn't have a good job, and at some point, my mom wasn't working at all. One day, I turned to my father and asked, "When are we going to get our own house?" I went out to the backyard and saw someone else's barbecue grill, and I said, "Someday, I want this in my house." I guess that's where it started for him. Since then, it was his mission in life to get a house for us. And now he has made it happen. That's something that he fulfilled for me—and we have a barbeque grill in the backyard!

FREE AND EASY

I have always pretty much taken things as they come. I don't look back too much, and I tend to go along with whatever happens to be in front of me. You can't choose everything that happens to you, but I try to take advantage of opportunities when they come my way. I just try to live life to the fullest. I don't really put labels on things, and I try not to judge others too much. I'm told that I am a good people person, and I try to focus on the people who are in my life.

I haven't had a chance to tell President Núñez yet, but I want her to know how much I appreciate the opportunity that she has provided me in this program. Being here at Eastern is a big positive factor in my life. I realize what an opportunity this is; many of the kids in my neighborhood, in my high school, don't have this opportunity. It's important for me and the other students in the program to take advantage of this chance to make something of our lives.

THE FUTURE

I am majoring in sport and leisure management. I want to be a physical therapist. After Eastern, I plan to go on to physical therapy school and get my license. I love seeing smiles on people's faces when you can make them feel better. Helping people get healthy again after an injury or something that has happened to them physically will be my way of taking care of them. That's what I want to do.

At the same time, I continue to be fascinated by ancient civilizations and the mysteries that surround them. One of the things that we talk about at Eastern is the importance of questioning the status quo, not settling for the simplest answer, and recognizing that history isn't static — new knowledge about the past is being discovered every day.

For instance, the Great Pyramid of Giza is an engineering accomplishment that defies logic; the precise carving of each granite block, how tightly they fit together, the lifting requirements—none of it can be explained based on what we know of the world forty-five hundred years ago. To build the Great Pyramid would have required that eight hundred tons of stone be moved a day, twelve blocks an hour, twenty-four hours a day, for twenty years. How did they do it?

I just read *Physics of the Impossible: A Scientific Exploration into the World of Phasers, Force Fields, Teleportation, and Time Travel*, by the Japanese physicist Michio Kaku. I am not saying that I believe in time travel or that aliens from another planet inhabited the Earth. But I have learned that the world is a better place when we ask questions, when we don't settle for easy answers. After all, did anyone in 1950 think that we would land men on the moon less than twenty years later? What would Thomas Edison say today about the laptop in my dorm room? What would Alexander Bell say about my iPhone? What other mysteries from the past will we uncover, and what will they tell us?

I don't know what the answers are, but that's okay. For now, I just want to keep reading, keep exploring. What I love about going to college at Eastern is that no one stops me and says that my ideas are crazy or that I should stop trying to find out more. The day that we stop asking questions is the day that someone else will be telling us what to believe. If we can learn more about the secrets of the past, we can definitely make a better life for people in the future.

*   *   *

Eshwar took the fall 2013 semester off but hopes to return soon to the Dual College Enrollment Program.

IV

A Model for Reform

TWELVE

A Model for Educational Reform

How Inner-City Students Can Succeed on Your Campus

> This program is a national model that should be replicated by multiple
> institutions because it works and really meets students' needs.
> — Estela López, member of Connecticut State Board of Education, sen-
> ior associate, Excelencia in Education

The preceding chapters have shared the life stories of six Dual College
Enrollment Program (DCEP) students at Eastern Connecticut State University. These students have courageously detailed the most intimate moments in their lives — some heartbreaking, some filled with hope — as they
have offered their perspective on being given the opportunity to earn a
college degree.

In their own words, these six students have told of family struggles, of
life on the streets, and of the challenges that some of them have faced as
new arrivals to this country. They have also shared the excitement and
pride that they experienced as they discovered their own potential on our
campus.

I hope that these stories have brought to life the transformation that
more than sixty DCEP students have experienced since the program began in 2008. Given opportunity and support, these six students and their
peers are demonstrating how personal resolve can overcome social and
cultural challenges that have presented a barrier to educational achievement for generations of inner-city youth. I could not be more proud of
them.

* * *

As the DCEP at Eastern Connecticut State University has taken hold, it has achieved several regional and national recognitions. In February 2010, the program was named by the College Board as a New England Regional Forum recipient of the first CollegeKeys Compact Innovation Award for "initiating innovative, effective best practices that help low-income students get ready, get in and get through college." In March 2011, the New England Board of Higher Education named the DCEP the 2011 recipient of the Robert J. McKenna Award for Program Achievement.

With these recognitions have come requests to share the DCEP story with organizations at conferences and meetings across the nation. The two questions people ask me most frequently are "How did you do it?" and "How can we replicate your success?"

Eastern has been fortunate—it is uniquely positioned to affect the lives of the students targeted for the DCEP program. Our campus is located in a small town that nonetheless has similar demographics to Hartford, Connecticut, thus serving as a perfect laboratory for student engagement in the community. The local satellite center of the region's community college is also conveniently located a short five-minute walk from Eastern's residence halls. It is an ideal environment in which to respond to a serious educational and social need with the partnership model that the university has developed.

Your own community, college campus, or state will not have identical needs or opportunities to those found in Hartford, Manchester, and Willimantic, Connecticut. However, the achievement gap exists in every state of the union, and every state has economically depressed populations, whether urban or rural. The need for greater access to higher education exists throughout the country, and colleges and universities have a responsibility and unique opportunities to increase access among disadvantaged students. Matching your own community needs with your campus resources is the first step in assessing your goals in developing on-campus programs to close the achievement gap.

LESSONS LEARNED

Chapter 5 lays out in detail the original cornerstones of the DCEP: pick students most appropriate for the program; immerse them in a residential campus environment; support their first semester with concurrent enrollment in community college remedial courses; provide them with the financial support essential to success; surround them with a comprehensive system of support services; and promote a culture of inclusion and diversity on campus. Those six principles remain critical to DCEP students' progress at the same time that they have been refined to enhance the program.

As the DCEP program has unfolded over the past six years, the lessons learned by Eastern and our partners can serve as guidance to others interested in pursuing similar programs on their own. What follows is an extended discussion of some of the more important discoveries that DCEP stakeholders have made.

Help students adapt their street skills to the campus. The first lesson to be learned in working with disadvantaged inner-city youth is that they have a different emotional base than students living in the safety of the suburbs, one that makes their experience on campus unique. Educational programs—especially those that take low-income urban students away from their home environments—must be sensitive to these differences and find ways to support them.

Students who grow up in Hartford and other cities have developed a set of noncognitive survival skills to manage difficult life circumstances. There is an extensive body of literature that describes such students as "resilient," focused on securing their external environment and managing their emotions before they can begin to grow intellectually. Achieving physical security and emotional stability in the city is not easy. Referring to children growing up in poverty, journalist Paul Tough writes, "Children who grow up in stressful environments generally find it harder to concentrate, harder to sit still, harder to rebound from disappointments and harder to follow directions. And that has a direct effect on their performance in school. When you're overwhelmed by uncontrollable impulses and distracted by negative feelings, it's hard to learn the alphabet."[1] As Eastern alumna and Laurel Hall/Nutmeg Hall director Julisa de los Santos says bluntly, "Maslow's hierarchy must be met. If they don't have food, shelter, and clothing, how can we expect kids to focus on their intellectual, ethical, and social development?"

The academic skill deficiencies that many of these students face—in language, mathematics, and other subject areas—can be overcome only once they are comfortable with their external surroundings. Building trust with people who are new to their lives, feeling secure in an unfamiliar environment, and reaching out to seek assistance are all new experiences for students coming to campus from the harsh realities of their urban neighborhoods.

Helping DCEP students adjust to their new experiences while respecting their sense of dignity is a fine line that must be negotiated. "These students don't want to be treated as charity cases," says Starsheemar Byrum, coordinator of the Women's Center and Intercultural Center.

> They tell us, "Treat me like other students; treat me so I know you value me." They don't want pity; they don't want to feel like an experiment. Being tough is a way to mask some of the issues and feelings they have. They are taught to respond to emotional issues in a detached way or it is too overwhelming. As we build trust, they are less de-

tached. And of course, they don't have a badge; they look and act like
everyone else. That's the comfort zone we want them to be in.

Sometimes getting comfortable is difficult, especially for students who
are hesitant to ask for help. As financial aid coordinator Gregory Ashford
explains,

> Some students are very reluctant to ask for help. I tell them, "If you
> don't ask and seek out help, you will be left alone." I tell them that
> vulnerability is not a bad thing; if they are willing to seek help, their
> success will help their community. I discovered one student couldn't
> find his family but he wouldn't tell me. So I had him apply as an
> independent student. Basically his parents were missing in action. He
> finally realized he couldn't do it himself and he started to get on the
> right track.

As DCEP students from Hartford and Manchester become comfortable in
their new environment, they are encouraged to adapt their street skills to
skills that they need to survive life on campus—meeting deadlines, working collaboratively, accessing resources, being self-motivated to attend
class, and being responsible at their on-campus jobs. Current DCEP coordinator Rick Hornung explains,

> Resilient students want to work, they want to collaborate. We need to
> reward their efforts—teamwork, hard work, completing assignments,
> being in class on time, helping other classmates, doing their homework.
> They have shown us they have the ability, motivation, and desire to get
> through high school under trying circumstances. Now they need to
> demonstrate that they have the skills needed in college—reliability,
> consistency, and collaboration.

"It takes a while for some of these students to realize they don't have to
worry about a stray bullet, a home invasion, being robbed, or confronting
gang warfare on our campus," says LaQuana Price, assistant director of
admissions.

> We want them to know they will be safe for four years. They can walk
> to class without fear; no one is going to steal their book bag. But it is a
> different world, and we know that, especially when a student says, "I
> don't bring books home, because I don't want anyone to know I am
> smart. Then I become a target."

Getting comfortable on campus can mean becoming uncomfortable in
one's own skin. The fall 2011 DCEP cohort discovered that when it took
an Improvisational Theater course together on Eastern's campus. "In any
theater course, you need to teach students it's personal but not 'personal,'" says theater instructor Alicia Bright-Holland.

> In the beginning, the students were hesitant, reticent to suggest im-
> provements to each other. But everything we do is about building trust.
> Actors take risks, knowing that people are there to help. As the stu-

dents developed community within the class, they got better. They developed their public speaking skills and improved their confidence. They learned that in acting, it's just you. There are no papers, no research. It's a journey, and I haven't had one student who hasn't grown in some way. Actors excavate a lot of their insides—it can be unintentionally therapeutic. The dual enrollment students saw it while it was happening, drawing from their life experiences both at home and on campus. It was a good way to bridge their two worlds.

Students must learn to live in two worlds. This "living in two worlds" is another critical aspect of the changes facing inner-city college students that campus officials need to address. Often the biggest challenge that DCEP students at Eastern face is dealing with the expectations of those they leave behind. The "tug" from home ranges from helping out their families—one student frequently sends earnings home from his on-campus job—to responding to friends who may be jealous of the progress that a DCEP student is making on Eastern's campus.

Quinebaug Valley Community College's Robert Fernandez explains that "there are certain societal pressures that occur within the family and the community. They see someone getting an education and growing as a threat. 'You're going to forget where you come from.' The family will ask 'why are you wasting your time with education? Why aren't you working?'"

Julisa de los Santos also notes the challenge that DCEP students have in balancing two different worlds:

> It is difficult for them to go from a street mentality to the campus; they are essentially living two lives. When they go back home, they need to reconcile those two lives. It's difficult for them to explain the changes that are occurring in their lives to their parents. Coming back to campus, they need someone to talk to, to help them figure out their new identity. They have to find the balance between keeping their culture while finding their place as a student on a college campus. The ones who bring their friends on campus are the ones who have a better, clearer understanding of who they are. The students who are worried about their "street cred" back home are more likely to be tempted.

At the same time that DCEP students are dealing with their double lives, the program's coordinators understand the need to counsel the students' families. As Amika Gomes, assistant director of the Academic Services Center at Eastern, notes,

> College is foreign to many of these families. They are not familiar with anything that occurs here. Some families understand the value of college, but still expect their students to send money home. And the students can feel the tension and a sense of isolation; they realize that not a lot of other students have these same issues.

Collaborating with the counselors at Hartford Public High School, East-ern's staff are working to counsel families without prior college experi-ence on the value of a college education so that they can be more suppor-tive of their students. In addition to parent meetings and family orienta-tions, university assistant Jennifer Holowaty worked with psychology faculty to develop and conduct a workshop for DCEP students on how to deal with and balance family pressures.

The DCEP team also recognizes the need to respect a student's family life and heritage. "These students do not want to lose their culture," says de los Santos. "We need to make sure that the academic experience we provide does not diminish that culture. We also need to appreciate that parents cannot provide the support we offer here. We need to build the student here, respecting their cultural identity while embracing the per-son they are becoming."

These two realities of urban students' lives—an emotional framework based on basic survival and the disconnect between their home and cam-pus lives—must be well understood when creating a successful college experience for disadvantaged students. As the narrative here describes, a clear understanding of the unique circumstances of college students from low-income minority families from our cities is as important as any prog-rammatic elements of a dual enrollment program. The development of trusting relationships, the personal counsel of faculty and staff, and a frank ongoing dialogue about the psychological and emotional chal-lenges these students are experiencing form a critical foundation for cog-nitive and intellectual development to take place.

Core program components reaffirmed. Beyond the critical need to under-stand that the psychological and emotional challenges facing inner-city college students must be met before academic progress can be made is the implementation of the core components of a successful on-campus program to increase college access for disadvantaged high school gradu-ates.

Regardless of the size of the campus or community, the location or nature of feeder high schools, or the relative gap in students' academic proficiency, the core elements of the DCEP program put into place five years ago at Eastern Connecticut State University have proven to be the right model. Combining on-campus residency, concurrent enrollment at a community college and four-year college, and an extensive system of formal and informal support has the best chance of giving students from disadvantaged backgrounds a safe learning environment and a vision of a different world from the streets on which they grew up. This reaffirma-tion has come not only from the lessons learned in the past five years but also by additional research conducted over that time. A review of those key lessons and current research can ideally prove useful to other col-leges and communities seeking to initiate programs to increase educa-tional access.

Living on campus is the core of a successful college access program. "Providing the residential aspect to get them out of situations where they could be distracted makes all the difference to these students," says Peter Rosa, program officer at the Hartford Foundation for Public Giving, one of the major benefactors of the DCEP program. Living on campus, DCEP students gain confidence in their intellectual skills as they widen their social circles and receive positive reinforcement for academic progress. In class, as members of campus clubs and organizations, and in their on-campus jobs, they learn self-discipline, responsibility, and professionalism.

Since Eastern began the DCEP program in 2008, a number of dual enrollment programs around the country have been reviewed by national researchers. Whereas dual enrollment programs have historically been offered to higher-achieving high school students, some of these programs are now targeting underrepresented populations.

An example of this is the Concurrent Courses initiative, which was a three-year dual enrollment program in California focused on high school career pathways, funded by the James Irvine Foundation, and managed by the Community College Research Center at Teachers College at Columbia University. The project supported eight programs involving ten colleges and twenty-one high schools from 2008 to 2010. Sixty percent of the approximately three thousand participating students were students of color and 40 percent spoke no English at home. The project's final report, released in July 2012, found that program participants, when compared with other students in their districts, were more likely to graduate from high school, more likely to transition to a four-year college rather than a two-year college, less likely to need remedial courses as college freshmen, and more likely to persist to their sophomore year in college and accumulated more college credits than peers not taking dual enrollment courses.[2]

In a related, earlier study, researchers Elisabeth Barnett of Columbia University and Liesa Stamm of Rutgers University indicated, "There is growing interest among advocates and policymakers in promoting dual enrollment opportunities for students traditionally underrepresented in higher education, including low-income, racially/ethnically diverse populations, and first-generation college-bound students."[3] Barnett and Stamm cite data from a City University of New York study indicating that low-income students, especially male students and those with lower grades, benefited more from dual enrollment courses than did their peers.[4]

Community College Research Center researchers do point to one dilemma facing dual enrollment programs for high school students. On the one hand, they argue that taking dual enrollment courses on a college campus is "the most authentic college experience," with students benefiting from various on-campus support services, and they provide data showing higher course completion rates for dual enrollment courses offered on a college campus.[5] Barnett and Stamm also indicate that "students earning dual credit from a two-year institution tended to get lower first-year GPAs than those earning dual credit at four-year colleges and universities."[6] On the other, they express concern that high school students do not have the transportation to commute to a college campus, and they suggest that staging the courses at the students' high schools would be less problematic.

If taking classes at a four-year college is a positive experience for a high school student but transportation to the college campus is an issue, then enrolling and housing these students on campus as college freshmen seems like a logical extension of the dual enrollment model. A postsecondary residential program such as Eastern's may be the best way to provide a college education to students from low-income families, especially those with academic skill deficits.

One other outcome of the DCEP experience at Eastern that reaffirms the importance of housing students on campus has been the recognition that students who participate in the program year-round are more likely to succeed. "Nothing good can come from them going back to their neighborhoods in the summer," says Christopher Dorsey, associate director of admissions. By making the program a twelve-month option for students who are willing to stay on campus throughout the year, the university can provide on-campus housing and summer jobs for DCEP students, who can also take summer classes and improve their chances of graduating on time.

Linking the remedial role of the community college and the four-year college campus experience is also a key to success in the first semester. The only other residential dual enrollment program that Eastern discovered in its research illustrates this important point. "Lowell Connections," a partnership between Middlesex Community College and the nearby University of Massachusetts–Lowell campus, has been operating for fifteen years. Students from area high schools who do not pass the university's entrance standards enroll at the community college for a year or more of remedial coursework. At one point, about 40 of the program's 250 students were housed at the university, even though all their coursework was at Middlesex, according to coordinator Charles Twomey. The housing experiment did not work—"The kids weren't mature enough. . . . They had financial problems and other issues"—and it has been discontinued. The differences between the Lowell model and Eastern's are instructive: in Eastern's DCEP program, students are taking classes simultaneously at both institutions; communications between the two schools takes place daily; each cohort is taking classes together and living in the same dormitory, which adds cohesion to their experience; and the smaller scale of the program is more manageable.

A combination of formal and informal mentors is critical to maintaining students' motivation and emotional well-being. Early on, Eastern's senior administrators provided one-on-one mentoring to DCEP students. While some benefited from the experience (see Federica Bucca, chapter 6), it became clear over time that students in the program were not universally comfortable. Coming from their humble backgrounds, some felt intimidated, and their previous experiences in high school implied, "You must be a real handful if they have you working with the top officials." Mentors were eventually recruited from throughout the Eastern campus, including hall directors, advisers, and other staff—especially those of African American and Latino heritage—who were likely to be familiar with the students' circumstances and issues.

Today, the formal mentors in the DCEP program are increasingly the students' work-study supervisors, the people they work for in their on-campus jobs. "It just makes more sense this way," explains Indira Petoskey, former DCEP coordinator and now assistant dean of continuing education. "The students see their supervisors on a regular, scheduled basis and it's in the supervisors' interests to monitor grades and make sure the students are succeeding academically."

Mentors—formally appointed or approached informally—must gain a student's trust before they can provide support. "The students tend to develop trust relationships with a single individual," says Starsheemar Byrum. "If that relationship ends or the person is reassigned, they feel physically alone again. They are very dependent on those relationships."

Psychology professor Margaret Letterman has become known for her ability to relate to DCEP students, both as a faculty member and as an informal mentor.

> We had a new student come in, and it took her a while to get comfortable. She finally came to me last week and I discovered she has no health insurance. Another student needed glasses and had no money, so I went to see our friends at the local Lions Club. A lot of the help we can provide comes informally. I cannot always help them myself, but I can usually find a way to refer them to someone who can.

Dean of Students Walter Diaz has taken a number of DCEP students under his wing.

> The relationships I build with these kids get pretty personal. Some of them don't have much of a home structure or family support. I will find situations where they are working on campus and giving the money over to their families to help support the household. I had one student's housing deposit provided by his pastor. The kids know they can reach me at any time. I give them my cell phone number so that they can catch me after hours, or after meetings. Sometimes when I see them on campus, I can see it in their face that they are dealing with an issue they need help on. They also know they can catch me at lunch. Sometimes, they need simple things like a ride home to Hartford. Or they need a meal. I ask them, "Have you eaten today?" Often they haven't had a meal, so I say, "Let's go get a bite to eat."

Sometimes the best counseling takes place in impromptu conversations. Kemesha Wilmot, a Hartford native and 2005 Eastern graduate, is now the coordinator of the Intercultural Center.

> When I see someone about to go home for the weekend, I tell them to enjoy the time with their families, but to bring their books home—"get your work done there, or go over to the public library and get away from the chaos at home." When I was at Eastern, I considered it as a sanctuary—away from the chaos of family, the chaos of the street. I tell them, "If you are successful, your family will be better off."

Start with the end in mind. Eastern is Connecticut's only public liberal arts university, and like most liberal arts institutions, the university community is proud of the broad-based intellectual skills that Eastern students gain during their time on campus—critical thinking, professional writing skills, the ability to work independently or in teams, and the ability to adapt to change. Even so, in today's world, students expect to learn marketable career skills so that they can participate in a highly competitive global job market.

Graduating from college with the confidence and ability needed to start a career is as important for DCEP students as it is for any other student on Eastern's campus. To that end, a number of career development strategies are used to support DCEP students' career goals. As is the case for all Eastern freshmen, DCEP students participate in career development programs in their dormitories, sponsored by the Center for Internships and Career Development and presented by peer counselors. In addition, career-related workshops are held especially for DCEP students, starting in the summer before they begin the program. As with all Eastern students, the goal is to have each student consider his or her interests and talents so that one can develop a career pathway and declare a major.

The on-campus jobs that DCEP students have not only provide additional income but also help them become more mature in their appearance and demeanor, teach them the importance of time management and being reliable, and introduce them to the professional workplace. In fall 2012, for the first time, three DCEP students were resident assistants, part of the staff responsible for the daily operations of three different resident halls. These are significant jobs and demonstrate the faith that the university is placing in these students. When DCEP students reach their junior and senior years, they also can participate in on- and off-campus internships that provide practical experience in job settings related to their majors.

Encourage students to become engaged in campus life. At Eastern, DCEP students can join one of more than seventy student clubs, play for a club or intramural team, or volunteer in the local community through the Center for Community Engagement. Eastern's data show that engaged students perform better academically: in fall 2012, students who partici-pated in clubs had an average 3.06 GPA and club officers, an average GPA of 3.16, compared to the overall university average GPA of 2.92.

Kemesha Wilmot explains the impact of club involvement on students in the DCEP program:

> I find that DCEP students who are involved in a student club adjust better to campus life than those who don't. I am the advisor for the FEMALES [Females Excelling, Maturing to Achieve Leadership, Excel-lence, and Success] club, and I find that students who get involved quickly find their comfort zone. They discover a place where they be-long, a group of other students whom they feel connected to. This is the first time they are away from their families and their neighborhoods — the familiar part of their lives. I also encourage them to get involved with the academic clubs associated with their majors.

Engaged students learn leadership skills as well. Financial aid coordina-tor Gregory Ashford offers one example as illustration:

> [Dual enrollment student] Jahaira Camacho is a leader in the Women's Center. She has accepted a leadership role in a situation where she is making a statement about a social condition — violence against wom-en — that makes her an activist by definition. To be an activist on a campus is not easy. She is holding her head high and making her voice heard. To be out in front is commendable; leaning into her discomfort and moving forward. That's how we all grow.

Don't lower your college's academic standards; raise the level of support given to disadvantaged students. As challenging as the issues are that inner-city students face in attempting to succeed on a college campus, they do not want to be treated as charity cases. The worst thing that can happen is for an institution to have a double standard in working with these students. Hartford Public High School's Charlene Senteio explains,

> It is important to give kids an honest appraisal of their academic per-formance. We need to tell them if they are reading at the fourth-grade level; they need to know the reasons why they are where they are. One student I was talking to was in his fifth year in high school, and had failed most of his courses. He thought the remedial courses didn't count, and I had to explain to him that he needed those because he needed help. "I have never been told that," he told me. We need to be more honest with the kids.

"These kids come from deficient schools and many simply aren't ready for college-level coursework, especially in mathematics," adds Margaret Letterman.

> Some of them got A's in high school and are barely C students here. It's easy to be an A student when the expectations and the curriculum are low. They have no idea. We need to be more honest with these kids. We

need to care about them enough to tell them what they need to do to be
successful, and stick around to help them get there.

From the top to the bottom. Ultimately, programs such as Eastern's DCEP
work only when the commitment to their success flows throughout the
organization, from the leadership to the lowest levels of the institution.
When we started developing the program in 2007, I knew that it would
fail if I was its only champion.

As Jeff Bartlett, college specialist at Hartford Public High School, said,

> at Eastern, Dr. Núñez's leadership and commitment have been funda-
> mental, but the buy-in has also been evident throughout the campus.
> The people at Eastern truly care about every individual and follow up
> with each one of them as they proceed through the program. You know
> the staff and faculty are committed when they can tell me how each
> student is doing in and out of the classroom years after they started.

LESSONS LEARNED: A FOUNDATION FOR SUCCESS

As the sixth year of the dual enrollment program at Eastern Connecticut
State University comes to a close, the university and its partners—Quinebaug Valley Community College and high schools in Hartford and Manchester—have benefited from the experiences of more than 60 DCEP students and the faculty and staff who have worked hard to support them
over the past five and a half years. We understand how important it is to
help low-income students from our cities become comfortable in the unfamiliar surroundings of a college campus. We have seen how taking
these students out of their home neighborhoods and surrounding them
with academic support, student services, and formal and informal mentors can help them gain confidence and progress academically. We have
noted the value of having concurrent enrollment at Eastern and Quinebaug Valley Community College during the students' first semester. We
have witnessed the personal maturity and intellectual growth that come
when students establish career goals and become involved in campus
activities. We also realize the importance of being honest with our students and the need for a campuswide commitment to the success of the
program.

Ultimately, the goal of education is to transform lives—to allow students to discover their inner potential, expand their perspectives, and
grow in ways that they might never expect.

> "This program speaks volumes when you are looking at the transfor-
> mation that takes place from the students' first day to the day of their
> graduation," says Amicah Gomes. "The early support in the first year
> is vital. At the same time, when you see juniors or seniors who still
> have mentors and still maintain their network, you realize that the

University's investment is a four-year commitment to helping those students meet their goals."

The results are worth this investment. As Quinebaug Valley Community College's Robert Fernandez describes, "through their experiences these students stop seeing poverty as an excuse. They see that they have the ability to compete and to complete school with kids from more privileged backgrounds than theirs. From their arrival at age eighteen to when they graduate as twenty-two- to twenty-three-year-olds, they are not the same person."

* * *

As I reflect on the transformation that continues to take place in the students in the DCEP at Eastern Connecticut State University, my thoughts wander back to the shacks of El Fanguito; to my first few words of English in Newark, New Jersey; to my parents' undying devotion to our family; and to my fortune in having Dr. Morris McGee for freshman English at Montclair State College. I think about the tobacco fields, thread mills, and munitions factories where the earliest Puerto Rican immigrants to Connecticut toiled and the tents, barns, and tenements in which they lived. I think about the socioeconomic barriers that continue to plague inner-city families, especially Latino and African American families. I ponder the achievement gap in Connecticut and the improbable fact that it is the largest in the country.

I recall with pride the first few days of the DCEP (more than six years ago) as we began planning for our first cohort of students. I listen to the stories of success and growth told by our DCEP students and by the faculty and staff who cheer them on each day. And I am gratified. The need is great, yet these students' potential is real. Every day that they get up to study on our campus is an opportunity for self-discovery.

We are on the right track: the students are thankful, and they are already giving back to our local community and their home neighborhoods. As we complete the DCEP's sixth year, we continue to graduate students, all the while seeking to improve the program's operations.

I hope in telling our story, we have given others the motivation to try a similar approach in their own communities and on their own campuses. The struggles facing the urban poor and the academic challenges that their conditions present to young people are found across our nation. Anything that we can do to stem that tide and begin to give low-income youth in our cities, especially Latino and African American students, hope for the future is worth our time and our investment.

If we approach this challenge with the same resolve for which America is known, and if we make full use of the resources at our disposal, we can transform the lives of individuals, of entire communities, and of our nation. If we do not, our future will not be as bright as our history has been nor as bright as the dreams that inspire us onward. This is the opportunity before us. Good luck on your journey!

NOTES

1. Paul Tough, *How Children Succeed: Grit, Curiosity, and the Hidden Power of Character*, quoted in book review, "School of Hard Knocks," by Annie Murphy Paul, *New York Times*, August 23, 2012, p. 3. Also see Kenneth R. Ginsburg, *Building Resilience in Children and Teens: Giving Kids Roots and Wings* (American Academy of Pediatrics, 2011), and *Resilience and Vulnerability: Adaptation in the Context of Childhood Adversities*, edited by Suniya S. Luthar (Cambridge University Press, 2003).

2. Katherine Hughes, Olga Rodriguez, Linsey Edwards, and Clive Belfield, "Broadening the Benefits of Dual Enrollment," Community College Research Center, Teachers College, Columbia University, 2011, pp. 8–40. Also see Concurrent Courses Initiative, http://www.concurrentcourses.org. For bibliography of publications based on the Concurrent Courses Initiative, see http://www.concurrentcourses.org/publications.html.

3. Elisabeth Barnett, senior research associate, Teachers College, Columbia University, and Liesa Stamm, senior research associate at Rutger University's Center for Children and Childhood Studies, "Dual Enrollment: A Strategy for Educational Advancement of All Students," Blackboard Institute, June 2010, p. 6.

4. Barnett and Stamm, "Dual Enrollment," p. 10.

5. Linsey Edwards, Katherine Hughes, and Alan Weinberg, "Different Approaches to Dual Enrollment," Community College Research Center, Teachers College, Columbia University; published in *Insights*, James Irvine Foundation, October 2011, p. 13.

6. Barnett and Stamm, "Dual Enrollment," p. 11.